FIRST TO DIE

FIRST TO DIE

The First Canadian Navy Casualties in the First World War

Bryan Elson

Formac Publishing Company Limited
Halifax, Nova Scotia

To Maxine and Christopher, with love.

Formac Publishing Company Limited recognizes the support of the Province of Nova Scotia through the Department of Tourism, Culture and Heritage. We acknowledge the financial support of the Government of Canada through the Canada Book Fund for our publishing activities. Formac Publishing Company Limited acknowledges the support of the Canada Council for the Arts for our publishing program.

Library and Archives Canada Cataloguing in Publication

Elson, Bryan
    First to die : the first Canadian navy casualties in the First World War/ Bryan Elson.

Issued also in an electronic format.
ISBN 978-0-88780-913-2

1. Canada. Royal Canadian Navy—History—World War, 1914-1918. 2. Midshipmen—Maritime Provinces—Biography. 3. Good Hope (Cruiser). 4. World War, 1914-1918—Casualties—Canada. 5. World War, 1914- 1918—Naval operations, British. I. Title.

VA400.E57 2010   940.4'5971   C2010-901147-3

Formac Publishing Company Limited
5502 Atlantic Street
Halifax, Nova Scotia
B3H 1G4
www.formac.ca

Printed and bound in Canada

Distributed in the United States by:
Casemate Publishers and Book Distributors, L.L.C.
908 Darby Rd,
Havertown, PA 19083

First published in the UK in 2011.

Distributed in the UK by:
Casemate UK
17 Cheap St.
Newbury, Berkshire
RG14 5DD

TABLE OF CONTENTS

PROLOGUE

"Then there arose in me the wish to build ships of my own like these some day, and when I was grown up to possess as fine a navy as the English." Such were the words of Kaiser Wilhelm II, Emperor of Germany, recalling his emotions after witnessing a review of the British fleet during one of his boyhood visits to his aunt, Queen Victoria of England. In later years he loved to wear his uniform as honorary Admiral of the Fleet in the Royal Navy.

Doubtless Wilhelm's personality played a role, but the impetus for a powerful navy stemmed from more fundamental causes. Since its victory over France in 1870 the new German Empire had become easily the strongest economic and military power in Europe. As a continental nation, with minimal dependence on overseas trade, the country had never felt it necessary to maintain a deep sea navy. But by the end of the 19th century Germany was taking part in the scramble for overseas colonies in which other European powers and the United States had been engaged since mid-century. Her lack of naval strength was soon perceived as a significant liability, as well as being inconsistent with her self-image as a world power, and she set out to build a navy 'second to none.'

Maintaining control of the sea was a matter of national life and death to Great Britain, totally reliant on seaborne trade, even for the food her population consumed. As the German challenge gathered weight she responded with her own ever-more expensive construction programme. From 1898 to 1914 the two countries devoted huge resources to building ever-increasing numbers of ever-more powerful ships, a contest that came to be known as the Anglo-German Naval Race, perceived in retrospect as being one of the fundamental causes of the First World War.

As the Royal Navy's margin of superiority inexorably narrowed, the mother country formally requested that the major colonies should begin to make a contribution to the naval defence of the Empire. In Canada, fierce political struggles ensued over whether the request should be met, and, if so, in what form. In May 1910 there emerged a Naval Service Act, creating a navy whose *matériel* consisted initially of two obsolescent British cruisers and the former Royal Navy dockyards in Halifax and Esquimalt.

There was one additional element, a college to train the future officers of the new-borne service. Established at Halifax, it opened its doors in January 1911 to the 21 young men from across the country who formed the first entry. Those who survived the First World War would preserve the navy through the interwar years and lead it through the Second.

Not all did survive. Four were to meet their deaths far from home at the very beginning of World War I, the first casualties of the infant Royal Canadian Navy. This is their story.

Chapter 1
BEGINNINGS

O n 11 January 1911, 21 young men from across Canada assembled outside the former naval hospital at the north end of the Halifax dockyard. They were the successful candidates in a competition to select the first intake of officers for the infant Royal Canadian Navy. They had been examined in November 1910, after responding to the following advertisement:

A competitive examination will be held in November next at the examination centres of the Civil Service Commission for the entry of Naval Cadets for the Naval Service of Canada. There will be twenty-five vacancies. Candidates must be between the ages of 14 and 15 years on the first of January next; must be British subjects and must have resided or their parents must have resided in Canada for two

years immediately preceding the examination, short periods spent abroad for the purpose of furthering one's education to be counted as residence. Successful candidates will join the Royal Naval College of Canada at Halifax in January next. The Course at the College is two years in length and the cost to parents including board, lodging, uniforms and all expenses is approximately $400 for the first year and $250 for the second. On parading out of college cadets will be rated Midshipman, and will receive pay at the rate of two dollars per diem. Parents of intending candidates should make application to the Secretary, Civil Service Commission, Ottawa, prior to October 16th next. Further information can be obtained on application to the Secretary, Department of Naval Service, Ottawa.

Class photo of the first entry to the Royal Naval College of Canada, January 1911. The College was established under the Naval Service Act, 10 May, 1910.

Unauthorized publication of this notice will not be payed for.

G.J. Desbarats
Deputy Minister of the Naval Service
Department of the Naval Service
Ottawa, August 1st, 1910.

Plans had moved with remarkable speed for a government bureaucracy. The Naval Service Act had come into effect in May 1910; by August arrangements were in place for selecting the first candidates; in November they were examined; and by January 1911 the first class reported to the college, which had received the designation "Royal" before it had even opened. Since the advertisement had not appeared in some newspapers until early October, many parents must have been hard-pressed to submit their sons' applications by the end of that month. It was as though there was a rush to make up for lost time, and indeed that was the case.

To keep up with the rapidly expanding German navy, the British government found it necessary to seek assistance from the dominions, such as Canada and Australia, which in the past had never contributed to the Royal Navy (RN) that protected them. The British Admiralty and many Canadians preferred that support to take the form of direct financial contributions to the construction of new battleships in the United Kingdom. On the other hand, a growing spirit of independence led other Canadians to prefer that Canada build its own.

This dispute was a visible symptom of the "colony or nation" question then coming to a head.

For the cadets assembled outside the old naval hospital on that January morning in 1911, a divided Canada's long and bitter struggle to respond to British pressure to support the RN, while at the same time foster its independence, seemed to be settled. The event that finally mattered occurred eight months before. On 4 May 1910, Liberal Prime Minister Sir Wilfred Laurier's Naval Service Act received Royal Assent after a stormy passage through a parliament deeply divided on party lines.

The Act rejected the idea of a direct financial contribution to the RN, and constituted an independent Canadian navy. Initially, it consisted of the dockyards at Halifax and Esquimalt, two cruisers and their crews on loan or transferred from the RN, and the new Royal Naval College of Canada, in which the 21 cadets were the first to enter. Modest beginnings, but a sense of unlimited possibility must have sustained and encouraged the cadets as they embarked on their new life.

The first tangible result of the Act was the arrival of HMCS *Niobe* in Halifax on 21 October 1912, the 107th anniversary of the Battle of Trafalgar. *Niobe* was met at the harbour entrance by the armed Coast Guard ship *Canada*, on board which the first six Canadian cadets were already being trained. *Niobe* was a 13-year-old armoured cruiser, displacing 11,000 tons, with a crew of approximately 700, and

The armoured cruiser HMCS Niobe, *the Canadian Navy's first ship, arrived in Halifax 21 October 1910. Already obsolescent, she was initially manned by Royal Naval personnel on loan to the new service.*

The navy's second ship, the light cruiser HMCS Rainbow, *entering Esquimalt Dockyard 8 November 1910. In the foreground the sloop HMS* Shearwater.

Before the establishment of the RNCC, the RCN's first six cadets trained for a year in the armed Coast Guard Ship Canada, *and transferred to* Niobe *on her arrival.*

a principle armament of 16 6-inch guns. At anchor off the dockyard the cruiser was an impressive sight to the uninitiated.[1] In truth, naval technology was advancing at such a pace that it was already obsolescent. A few days later, the smaller, older, and even more out of date *Rainbow* arrived in Esquimalt. No doubt several of the prospective college cadets witnessed *Niobe*'s arrival. Of the 21, eight were from the Maritimes, including five from Halifax.

At the Imperial Conference in spring 1911, the admiralty agreed to the creation of a sector on each coast in which Canada was to exercise peacetime operational control of these ships. In the event of war, the Canadian government would decide when and which ships would be placed under admiralty control; once assigned, control remained with the RN for the duration.

The role of any armed service basic training is to inculcate entrants into the discipline and culture of their service, and to provide them with a basic knowledge of their profession. In the case of the RNCC, the educational objective was to prepare cadets for their naval careers. Here they were to learn both to obey and to command, in an atmosphere that fostered the development of an honourable character, promoted physical and mental fitness, and emphasized self restraint and self reliance.

Since 1878, Canada had a military cadet school, the Royal Military College (RMC) at Kingston, Ont. In 1910, staff from the embryonic RNCC visited RMC to observe its training methods, but there seemed to be no question then of combining the two colleges, which occurred in later years.

The most pertinent model for the RNCC, indeed for the overall development of junior officers, was the Royal Navy, from which the naval portion of the RNCC staff was entirely drawn. Inevitably, British practice was deeply embedded in the Canadian

The RNCC curriculum and exams mirrored those of the Royal Navy's training college HMS Britannia. Cadets received a broad education in both seamanship and engineering.

system. In both countries the naval colleges were specialized boarding schools, and parents paid the entire cost of their sons' educations. These costs were set high, supposedly to encourage students to work harder under pressure from home. Inevitably, the expense severely limited the pool of potential applicants and contributed to the impression that the naval officer corps was based on social class, an idea that was more acceptable in Britain than in Canada.

Unlike British cadets, who joined at 13, the Canadian intake was between 14 and 16 years of age. British cadets trained at Osborne and Dartmouth for four years, rather than the two years mandated at the RNCC. Graduates from both systems went to sea at approximately the same age, 17 years, and streamed together in an RN training cruiser for the next stage of their training.

RNCC staff consisted of naval personnel and civilians, the former on loan either from the RN or recently transferred to the fledgling RCN. The first commandant was Captain E.H. Martin, who was for a time the senior Naval Service officer in Halifax. He was a somewhat remote figure to the cadets. Their most important authority figure was the Senior Lieutenant, E.A.E. Nixon. Stern but fair, Nixon was to become the second commandant and the heart of the college during its later tribulations. The senior academic was Instructor Captain Hartley, the Director of Studies, well qualified thanks to previous service on the Dartmouth staff. Other academic staff came both from Britain and

The new RNCC, housed in the former Royal Naval hospital at the north end of the Halifax dockyard.

from local recruitment of Canadians. The overall ratio of staff to students was much higher than in ordinary secondary school.

Initial plans considered constructing the college in the dockyard. When this proved impractical, it was decided to use the former RN hospital at the north end of the yard. After renovations, this building provided accommodations and classrooms that were spartan but adequate. One of the first lessons instilled was the overriding requirement for neatness and cleanliness of person, uniform, and dormitory, impressed upon cadets at every turn by all members of the staff. What seemed like nitpicking was necessary and translated to their later circumstances in the cramped and crowded conditions of the ships where the cadets eventually served.

Royal Navy policy at this time held that in initial training engineering and seaman officers followed the same courses, only separating later into their specialties. Thus, theoretical and practical engineering, science, physics, mechanics and mathematics figured largely in the curriculum. Cadets were also instructed in English, French and history, with particular emphasis on naval history. They learned the basics of navigation and seamanship, and their studies were rounded out with physical training, drill, and boat work under oars, sail and power. Periodic tests and term exams were normal for all subjects. By achieving high marks the cadets earned advanced seniority on later promotion to the rank of lieutenant.

At this early stage of the cadets' careers, the five warrant officers and chief petty officers assigned to the college were crucial figures. They were specially selected for their maturity and their professional skills because their situation was in many ways difficult. Destined in a few years to be inferior in rank to their pupils, they were nevertheless expected to exert firm control in the training environment, knowing that the college experience was of critical importance to these future senior officers, perhaps faced with life and death decisions.

The RNCC held no official opening ceremony. In April 1911, Rear-Admiral Sir Charles Kingsmill made an inspection after which he expressed his thorough appreciation for everything that had been done. Kingsmill, borne in Guelph, Ont., had made a successful career in the RN. On retirement he returned to Canada and when invited to be the first head of the Naval Service in 1910, he accepted without hesitation.

As noted, the RNCC cadet programme consisted of two years at the College and one year at sea. Each college year was divided into two 20-week terms, with six weeks of leave between each pair. These long leaves were deliberately built in to permit cadets from the west to make the long train journey home and back, a trip lasting one week in each direction for those from British Columbia. Rather than face the expensive journey, many westerners no doubt chose to spend at least one leave with relatives or new-found friends in the east.

There was no greater sin for cadets than dead time. The day began at 6:35 a.m. with a compulsory cold bath, followed in summer by boat work and in winter by physical training, then a welcome breakfast. After inspection, classes began at 9:00 a.m. and ended at 4:00 p.m., with a break for lunch and drill. Before supper, cadets took part in compulsory games, including soccer, cricket, and hockey. After supper they were again inspected. An hour of compulsory study followed from 7:00 to 8:00 p.m., and an hour of free time before prayers, lights out, and bed at 9:00 p.m. Punctuality was demanded at every point, and every movement was carried out at the double.

Canadian-born Rear-Admiral Sir Charles Kingsmill became the first head of the new navy after a career in the RN.

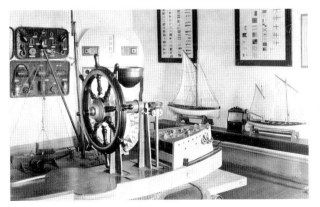

Seamanship instruction room; basic training with a model of a ship's wheelhouse.

TOP: *Weary but triumphant cutter racing crew.* MIDDLE: *Compulsory walk around Bedford Basin, mimicking boat pulling.* BOTTOM: *Later in compulsory walk, a less energetic group awaiting train at Prince's Lodge.*

Although there was no senior term, the January 1911 entry was divided into two groups, with a cadet captain appointed for each one. When the second entry joined in January 1912, the normal hierarchy of cadet captains, senior class and junior class was established, but the RMC tradition of hazing new entries did not spread to the RNCC. Discipline for minor infractions was enforced by the cadets themselves. Each week they received 75 cents pocket money from funds deposited by their parents, and minor fines could be levied against this amount.[2]

The RNCC had a sailing vessel, the 2-masted schooner *Diana,* which in summer embarked small groups of cadets for cruises along the intricate Nova Scotia coast, practical experience that included frequent groundings. On 24 May each year, the cadets entertained the belles of Halifax at a picnic on McNabs Island, chaperoned by the wives of the college staff.

A sporting highlight occurred when the college pulling crew was victorious over the junior officers of the visiting cruiser HMS *Carnarvon* in a cutter race. A photo shows the exhausted rowers slumped over their oars, with coxswain William Palmer standing in the stern sheets. For this achievement each rower was presented with a small replica silver oar.

At this remove, the personalities of the first 21 cadets are only dimly visible. The marks they made in their examinations, who were selected cadet captains, and their physical descriptions survive; but little is known of their personalities, still under development in their teenage years. The class included most of those who persevered through the lean years of the RCN during the 1920s and 1930s, and who led the navy through World War II. Among them were future Vice-Admiral G.C. Jones,

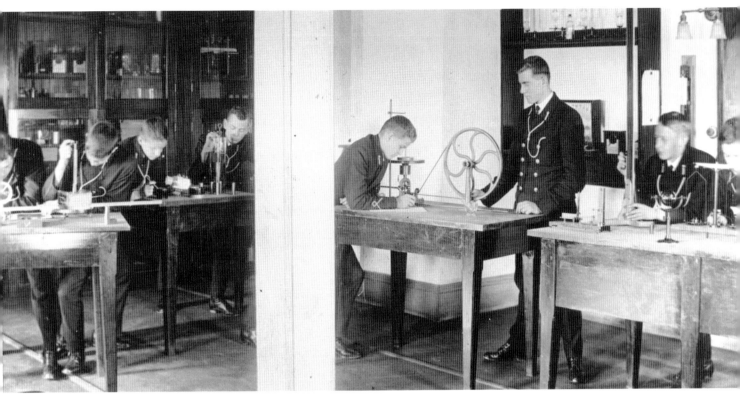

Practical instruction, electrical workshop.

Chief of the Naval Staff after 1943; and Rear-Admiral L.W. Murray, who commanded the Canadian Northwest Atlantic area from 1943 to the end of the Battle of the Atlantic. The end note[3] to this chapter contains nominal lists of the original CGS Canada cadets and the first RNCC entry.

Five of the first 19 graduates did not survive World War I, a casualty rate of more than 20 percent, seldom matched in any navy. One of the five, Lieutenant William M. Maitland-Dougall of Victoria, B.C., was in command of the British submarine D3, when it was misidentified by a French airship and sunk without survivors in March 1918. The other four died in 1914, before their twentieth

birthdays, the very first casualties of the infant RCN and, in fact, the first combatants of any Canadian service to be killed in action in World War I. Their names were Malcolm Cann, Victor Hatheway, William Palmer and Arthur Silver.

Unfortunately, Victor Hatheway's service records cannot be located, but those of the other three are in the National Archives in Ottawa. They contain the bare facts of two years of cadet training, together with a few vignettes that allow the four young men to emerge as individuals, if only dimly.

By coincidence, the four were all Maritimers. The youngest was John Victor Hatheway, 16 in 1911, born in Granville, N.S., but residing with his family in Fredericton, N.B. when he joined. Next in age was Malcolm Cann, also 16, the son of a prosperous ship owner and merchant of Yarmouth, N.S. William Palmer, 17, was from Halifax, the son of a sergeant-major in the Royal Canadian Engineers, an interesting exception to the upper-middle class status of most of the cadets' families. The second Haligonian was Arthur Silver, whose father, Captain Harry St. Clair Silver, was a veteran of the 1885 Riel Rebellion and a well-known Halifax businessman.

Each cadet's application was endorsed by a Guarantor. In the case of Cann and Palmer these were, respectively, the principals of the Yarmouth and Halifax Academies, while Silver's was signed by the head of the Church of England Institute in Halifax.

At the new entry medical examination, none of the three met the minimum chest measurement of 32 inches. Their files contain a letter from the Director of the Naval Service informing their parents of this fact, but each cadet was allowed to remain in college with the hope that regular exercise and physical training would correct this defect. Since all graduated, presumably it was corrected, although Malcolm Cann's mess jacket, preserved in the Yarmouth Museum, is remarkably small.

William Palmer as infant, schoolboy and cadet. His father was a sergeant-major in the Royal Canadian Engineers.

As their studies progressed the cadets were keenly interested in anything affecting the development of the new national navy, borne as it was after a fierce political struggle. Youthful as they were, the cadets must have been aware that politics might continue to play a major role in determining the wisdom of their choice of careers.

Career satisfaction depended in part on the quantity and quality of the ships on which the new officers would serve. In 1911-1912 the outlook was exciting. The Laurier government requested tenders to build in Canada a fleet to consist of one *Boadicea* class heavy cruiser, four smaller *Weymouth* class vessels, and six destroyers. It was later decided that *Niobe* would be retained and take the place of the proposed heavy cruiser. Buying from established British yards would have been cheaper and quicker, but fostering a Canadian shipbuilding industry was a desirable by-product of the programme, on both economic and political grounds. The industrial capability had to be created, so the government promoted the establishment in Montreal of the British firm of Vickers Ltd., to be known as Canadian Vickers. These decisions meant that construction would take six rather than three years. Nevertheless, the

Niobe *in dry dock, showing hull damage sustained in grounding on Nova Scotia's south shore. Taken by Cadet Malcolm Cann, who was aboard at the time.*

ships would be well on their way by the time the cadets completed their training. In these heady days, their morale must have been high. It soon received a serious jolt.

Admiral Kingsmill wanted the *Niobe* to concentrate on afloat training for the new recruits now joining the service. Unfortunately, he was unable to resist pressure for the ship to make a visit to Yarmouth, N.S., in the summer of 1911, to enhance the political interests of a local Member of Parliament. Because of adverse weather the visit was not a success from a political or any other standpoint. Cadet Malcolm Cann, on leave at his family home and with commendable keenness, seized the chance to join the cruiser for the return voyage to Halifax.

On the night of 30–31 July, *Niobe* ran aground on Southwest Ledge off Cape Sable. One engine room flooded and one propeller was lost. Wireless requests for assistance were transmitted and preparations were made to abandon ship. After about two hours *Niobe* floated clear and anchored, while the crew struggled desperately to keep it afloat. The cruiser HMS *Cornwall*, hastening to help, grounded briefly in fog, but was able to refloat and tow *Niobe* to Halifax, where it entered dry dock for repairs. The RN navigation officer was severely reprimanded and dismissed the ship, and the officer of the watch was reprimanded.

In practical terms, Cadet Cann no doubt learned more about the hazards of navigation and the importance of damage control on that night than he did during his whole college course. But the accident had wide-reaching effects. *Niobe*'s ignominious return under tow provided opponents of the naval policy with a golden opportunity to ridicule the whole idea of a Canadian navy. Even William Palmer's former classmates at the Halifax County Academy noted in their yearbook "William Archibald Palmer … left us at Christmas to join Ye Mariners of England at the Naval College, and we hear he is learning to steer the Niobe clear of rocks."

The expensive repairs took 16 months, during which time recruiting virtually ceased and many of the men loaned from the RN returned home.

Ironically, in August 1911, consent was granted to add the prefix "Royal" to the name of the infant service. To the naysayers the distinction appeared incongruous, given that the newly minted Royal Canadian Navy's only apparent achievement was to have run aground half its ships. In the same month, the RNCC received a vice-regal visit from Governor-General, the Duke of Connaught, but as the cadets were on leave he simply toured the facilities.

When the cadets returned to the college for their second term in the early fall of 1911, prospects seemed dimmer than only a few months before. A general election was held in September. The major campaign issue was Laurier's intention to negotiate free trade with the United States, but the unpopularity of his naval policy also played

Another view of Niobe's *damaged hull.*

a role. Whatever political convictions the cadets had, they must have recognized that a defeat for Laurier would not bode well for them. In fact, Laurier was defeated by Sir Robert Borden's Conservatives, and the cadets and the navy as a whole waited in trepidation to learn his intentions.

With Laurier's defeat, John Hazen, a former premier of New Brunswick, became Minister of Marine and Fisheries. Rear-Admiral Kingsmill continued as Chief of the Naval Service. Prime Minister Borden had made up his mind that the RCN as envisaged by Laurier was completely inadequate. In the increasingly tense international situation, he believed that the country's security depended on making a direct contribution to the RN. In exchange, he hoped that Canada would have a voice in determining the foreign and defence policy of the British Empire. His policy was strongly influenced by his close relationship with Winston Churchill, who became First Lord of the Admiralty in 1910. As a first step, Borden did not award the contracts for vessel construction planned under Laurier's policy. In December 1911, he confirmed his intention to repeal the Naval Service Act but did not announce a replacement policy.

It was in this atmosphere that the first RNCC entry wrote their year-end examinations. Morale among staff, students, and parents must have suffered from the uncertainty. The once promising new navy was likely to be limited to *Niobe* and *Rainbow* for the foreseeable future, and even that was doubtful since *Niobe* still languished in dry dock. For the moment at least, the college continued to be funded, parents continued to pay the fees, and instruction proceeded.

In January 1912, ten cadets of the second entry joined the college, and the first 21 experienced a heady sense of enhanced prestige relative to the

Niobe under repair in dry dock, Halifax, autumn 1911.

19

rookies. The relentless daily routine ensured that the cadets had little time to brood on their futures. It is tempting to believe that they were unconsciously absorbing what became the RCN's characteristic defence mechanism: fatalistic acceptance, coupled with a stubborn determination to make the best of whatever resources a grudging and uninterested country saw fit to provide.

Borden's commitment to direct support of the Royal Navy intensified Canadian interest in the Anglo-German naval race. It was a time of rapid technological change. Both navies experimented with submarines and aircraft. The advent of the

would be fought at relatively short ranges. For this reason, battleships were armed with the largest possible number of guns of all calibres, enabling them to plaster their opponents with rapid fire. The British were the first to act on the realization that improvements in projectiles and fire control permitted a ship principally armed with large calibre guns to stand off at long range and target the enemy with heavy shells. Smaller calibre weapons might never come within range. Under the pressure of Admiral Sir John "Jacky" Fisher, and in conditions of extreme secrecy, Britain rapidly constructed HMS *Dreadnought*, the first all-big-gun

Dreadnought type battleships. Left to right: SMS Kaiser, USS Michigan, *HMS* Dreadnought.

torpedo promised to influence tactics in as yet unknown ways. But the decisive weapon continued to be the battleship, organized in fleets that both sides assumed would someday meet in a tremendous encounter that would decide the outcome of any war between the two powers. Each new class of battleship, on one side or the other, boasted heavier armour and increased firepower, forcing the opponent to leapfrog to a new class in an increasingly expensive competition.

In 1909, the British made a daring innovation that temporarily gave them a decisive advantage. For years it was accepted that fleet engagements

battleship. In another innovation, this ship was driven by turbines rather than reciprocating engines, which achieved higher speeds and greater reliability. Existing battleships of all countries were immediately rendered useless, except against each other or smaller vessels.

The *Dreadnought's* new capabilities required a great increase in tonnage. To match her with their own dreadnought-type vessels, the Germans had to construct much larger ships, but these would no longer be able to navigate the Kiel Canal, through which vessels were transferred between the Baltic and North Seas. The Germans were forced to undertake the widening and deepening of the canal at enormous expense. They accepted the challenge without hesitation, work began, and the building race never slackened.[4]

In January 1912, as the RNCC cadets began their second year of instruction, the British sent a mission to the Kaiser to press for a mutual slowdown in the speed of new construction. The request was refused. The German programme continued at the average rate of two-and-one-half dreadnought battleships commissioned in each of the next six years, 15 new vessels by 1918. By 1914, the expansion of the Kiel Canal would be completed, allowing Germany to concentrate its High Seas Fleet for a North Sea sortie at very short notice, when refits or detachments to other theatres had temporarily reduced the strength of the British Grand Fleet. To maintain a comfortable margin in the critical area, the British needed to build at an average rate of four-and-one half battleships per year, or 27 over the six-year period. Any contribution that an increasingly prosperous Canada could make to this enormous effort was critical.

In June 1912, Borden and Hazen travelled to London for consultations, followed up in August by a secret memorandum from Churchill to Borden, requesting Canada to finance three new dreadnoughts,

Liberal Sir Wilfred Laurier (left) and Conservative Sir Robert Borden (right). Their fundamental differences on Canada's naval defence left the country totally unprepared on the outbreak of the First World War.

additional to the planned British programme. In October, the Canadian cabinet approved the plan, which triggered the resignation of Borden's Quebec lieutenant. On 12 December 1912, Borden introduced his Naval Aid Bill in the House of Commons, providing for the funding by Canada of three modern battleships, at a total cost of $35,000,000. To be named *Acadia*, *Quebec*, and *Ontario*, these ships would be transferred to Canada after sufficient Canadians had been trained.

Laurier remained committed to the idea of a Canadian navy and denied that a naval building emergency existed. His Liberals vehemently fought the Naval Aid Bill, using every debating trick of delay and filibuster. At times it seemed that MPs might even come to blows on the floor of the House of Commons.

The results of the political wrangling in Ottawa were visible in the naval ports. Recruiting virtually ceased and the number of desertions exceeded the number recruited. *Niobe* and *Rainbow* had about half their complements, and the former was still confined to harbour.

It required a great deal of faith to persevere in these circumstances. No doubt the issue of the naval race and Canada's involvement was an active topic of discussion, and the college copies of the authoritative annual *Jane's Fighting Ships* would be

Front row: Malcolm Cann (centre); Arthur Silver (right). Second row: John Victor Hatheway (second from left). Rear row: William Palmer (second from left); William Maitland-Dougall, fifth to die in the First World War (third from left).

frequently consulted. The service they had joined with such high hopes was now the source of bitter national divisions. Political debates were actively discouraged, but from a purely professional and career standpoint, the cadets must have compared Borden's Royal Navy big ship plan with Laurier's Canadian navy small ship concept. There is no telling which they preferred; perhaps they were as divided as the country. In any case they had more important things to think about. By Christmas, they learned the results of their final examinations and the seniority their performance might have earned them.

During his first year Cann suffered from tonsillitis and was for a time under threat of expulsion for lack of progress in mathematics; but in the end he

The 20 graduates of the first entry, probably taken aboard HMCS Niobe before the newly minted midshipmen sailed for England.

passed out of the college with a Third Class standing, number 15 out of 19, his 19 out of 19 in engineering somewhat offset by being eighth in pilotage, with the remark "very good indeed" on the record. According to Captain Martin, his "general conduct and attention to his studies have been very good indeed." His classmate John Grant remembered him as "a good messmate from Yarmouth, Nova Scotia."[5]

Palmer also suffered from tonsillitis, but was the academic star of the first entry. He finished first out of the 19, with a First Class certificate and four months of earned seniority. He took top marks in the final examinations in engineering, mathematics, physics, chemistry and pilotage. Captain Martin's personal remarks were identical to those on Cann's certificate. According to John Grant, Palmer was "very brainy, used to be top of the class apparently without having to work."

Silver graduated 13 of 19, with a Second Class certificate and two months seniority. He received "Very Goods" in engineering, seamanship, and pilotage; but his English was rated "Poor." Again, Captain Martin affixed his standard remark, with the added notation "... and has made an excellent

Cadet Captain." Grant remembered him as a keen fisherman from a well-known Halifax family, and as being rather like Hatheway, whom he characterized as "very fine looking, modest, very nice, played the piano for our sing songs, a promising young officer."

These three cadets were similar in physical appearance. Cann and Silver were five feet seven inches tall, and Palmer exceeded them by a mere half inch. All three had blue eyes. Cann was fair-haired and the other two dark-haired. As previously noted, Hatheway's records have disappeared. His academic performance is unknown, and apart from Grant's remarks his personality can only be guessed at from his photographs.

Graduation represented a milestone, which no doubt relegated the naval controversy into the background, at least temporarily. Effective 25 January 1913, the 19 graduates of the first entry were appointed to the RN training cruiser HMS *Berwick*, in which they would undergo their next training stage towards commissioned officer status. For the first time they received pay, at the rate of two dollars per day.

There was time for only a short leave. Then came the much-anticipated day when they embarked on the liner *Tunisian* for the passage to England. The world opened before them and, again, all things seemed possible. On their transatlantic passage, the high-spirited youngsters travelled first class, even if they were mere midshipmen, a taste of their enhanced status. It was a rough passage and several spent most of it fighting seasickness, only dispelled as the coast of Ireland came into view. At 5:00 p.m. the next day, the ship berthed at Liverpool. The arrival of the first prospective Canadian naval officers was noteworthy enough that a group

photograph was taken in the *Tunisian*'s lounge for one of the local newspapers.

Immediately afterwards, they boarded the Euston Special, a crack train, which carried them to London at speeds of up to 70 miles per hour. Ensconced in a private car, they had first use of the diner, always important to healthy young men; so important to Malcolm Cann that he sent his mother a copy of the menu! In the dark they saw little of the countryside, but marvelled at the toy-like engines and carriages of British railways, which Cann dubbed "cute." Arriving at Euston Station, they spent what remained of the night in the nearby Endsleigh Hotel. At 10:30 a.m. the next day, they entrained for the 30-mile journey to Chatham, the RN base at the mouth of the Thames River.

Chapter 2
THE UNCERTAIN TRUMPET

Upon reaching Chatham, the midshipmen reported aboard HMS *Berwick*, which was to be their home for the next year. Captained by Sir John Clinton-Baker, *Berwick* was a Bristol class cruiser, weighing 9,800 tons, mounting 14 6-inch guns, and with a maximum speed of 23 knots. Its present role was on-the-job training of junior officers. The Canadians might have for the first time mingled with their RN counterparts, graduates of Osborne and Dartmouth. But according to John Grant, the British midshipmen were all sent to other training cruisers, *Cumberland* or *Cornwall*. By accident or design, the "wild colonial boys" were concentrated in *Berwick*, where they formed what Grant called "a very happy, a very lively gunroom."

Nevertheless, through reciprocal hospitality and sports the two groups became acquainted with each other. Some wariness was inevitable. All were about the same age, but the British had two more years of naval indoctrination and many were descended from long lines of distinguished naval officers, and on the whole probably originated from a higher social stratum. It did not help that the Canadians were better paid. No doubt there were muttered references to "bloody colonials." In time, the same rigorous training programme and shared experiences ashore and afloat smoothed many differences, leaving at worst a two-way attitude of amused tolerance and at best, in many cases, the beginnings of long-term friendships.

Although they did not know it, the 21 midshipmen of the first RNCC entry established a pattern of Canadian junior officer training with the RN that lasted for nearly 50 years, influencing the character of the RCN even to the present time, for better or for worse.

The position of midshipman (mids) was steeped in naval history. Until the late Middle Ages, no real

Unidentified midshipmen fighting seasickness on the quarterdeck of HMS Berwick.

distinction between warships and merchant vessels existed. When danger threatened, merchant vessels were hired or requisitioned with their crews, and soldiers were drafted aboard to do the actual fighting. The ship's master handled the vessel as directed by the soldiers' commanding officer, who remained ignorant of the seamanship involved.

As cannon were adapted for use at sea, it became important to carry the maximum number of guns, sacrificing most of the space hitherto used for cargo. The new purpose-built warship led to a permanent fighting navy maintained at public expense in both peace and war.

Despite this revolution, old distinctions persisted between the mariners who sailed ships and the gentleman who fought them. "There were seamen and there were gentlemen in the navy ... but the seamen were not gentlemen, and the gentlemen were not seamen." Since gentlemen were born and not made, it was inconceivable that a seaman could be turned into a gentleman. The solution was to turn gentlemen into seamen, by sending suitable young men to sea to acquire essential technical knowledge.

The rate of midshipman originally belonged to a petty officer in charge of the midships area of the upper deck. Aspiring young gentlemen were to be paid at the same rate and, with the passage of time, they assumed the title as well. On the job training was emphasized, but they were expected to assume important leadership roles, in command of ships' boats and parties of men, and in charge of a section of guns in battle. This system proved itself over the years and, with some alterations, still prevailed in 1914, indeed for long afterwards.

Midshipmen were not commissioned officers. For the last time in their careers, they took advantage of a less rigid relationship with other ranks to gain some insight into the outlook of the men of the lower deck. The opportunity was a mixed blessing. Canadian society produced a seaman whose attitude and background differed significantly from his British counterpart. Leadership approaches learned in the RN did not necessarily translate well to the RCN of later years.

The term "snotty" was widely used as a synonym for midshipman. It was reflected in their uniform jackets, which had three buttons on each cuff, supposedly to discourage them from wiping their noses on their sleeves. A senior lieutenant-commander had responsibility for their overall development and conduct; inevitably, he was referred to as the snotties' nurse.

Each midshipman was required to keep an illustrated journal, in which he recorded highlights of the ship's programme, with descriptions of ports visited and significant events in the training schedule. Once a week, the journals were submitted for

Canadian mids in Berwick. *In the centre, front row, seated, the 'snotties' nurse'.*

examination by the snotties' nurse, who was rarely satisfied. Stoppage of leave was often employed as a motivator.

Two mids were assigned in rotation to do duty as "doggies" for the captain and commander (the executive officer in modern terms). This unflattering term accurately described their roles, which were to attend on their master at all times in case it occurred to him to dispatch them on some errand.

Messages were politely but bluntly expressed, along the lines of, "My compliments to the Commander (E), and would he kindly stop making black smoke from the after funnel," which the unfortunate doggy was obliged to repeat verbatim, standing rigidly at attention before the senior officer, "Commander's compliments, sir, and would you kindly stop making black smoke from the after funnel." The job mostly involved prolonged periods of standing

TOP: *Navigation was a critical skill. Here unidentified mids use sextants to measure the sun's altitude from* Berwick's *deck.* BOTTOM: *The protected cruiser HMS* Berwick, *lightly armoured and mounting 14 6-inch guns. A training ship in peacetime.*

at ease outside their masters' cabins, interrupted by frantic searches for the intended recipient of the message.

Midshipmen slung their hammocks in mess decks. They were members of the gunroom mess, a training version of the commissioned officers' wardroom mess. Here the esoteric manners and customs of wardroom life were inculcated under the watchful eye of the sub-lieutenant of the gunroom, a powerful figure in the tiny closed society. He had the authority to administer six strokes of his cane on the backside of any of his charges who contravened the sometimes fuzzy rules. According to John Grant, the sub-lieutenant did not hesitate to use that authority, but the recipient usually felt that he received what he deserved, and then the incident was over. A temporarily painful mark on his anatomy was much better than a permanent mark on his record. Alcohol was available under strictly controlled conditions, and the young men learned by example or punishment how to handle it responsibly.

Midshipmen were expected to be high-spirited and mischievous, but there was a line between transgressions that were semi-tolerated and those attracting serious disapproval. Where the line lay was usually discovered by painful experience. Midshipmen were also expected to make mistakes. Again, there was a line between the honest error, made in good faith, and the error perceived as arising from character defects or the lack of officer-like qualities.

From the moment of joining, midshipmen were impressed with the importance of learning the location and purpose of the ship's numerous compartments, a sea-borne rabbit warren: "Know your ship" was the constant cry. For weeks trainees moved from deck to deck, filling in the designations of every space shown on their diagrams of the ship. The process worked and became second nature, one they repeated in a less structured way, but as a matter of course, in every new ship in which they served.

Spaces aboard the *Berwick* were converted to classrooms. The curriculum aboard *Berwick* closely resembled the training college's, but, with an increased emphasis on practical application in actual conditions at sea. The cadets rotated in small groups through the various departments of the ship: engineering, supply, gunnery, and the rest, temporarily integrated to the extent possible, absorbing the atmosphere of the different specialties. The main point of the exercise was not so much to learn the minutiae of the various departments, as to recognize that they must work together as a team to create an effective fighting unit.

Based at Plymouth, *Berwick* first worked up with the Home Fleet. From March to September of 1913, the ship circumnavigated the coast of the British Isles, touching at 15 ports in Wales, Ireland, Scotland, and England. In most places *Berwick* anchored, and there was a great deal of boat traffic between ship and shore. As part of their training, midshipmen took charge of the boats, a challenging task in bad weather or when bringing off a large body of inebriated liberty men in the dead of night. Many were the scrapes and dents on the immaculate hulls, and many were the furious dressing downs and stoppages of leave to encourage the mids to become more skilful.

Early on, the cadets were introduced to the great curse of naval life in that era, coaling ship. Virtually all warships were driven by steam, generated in vast boilers by the burning of coal. As First Lord, the energetic Winston Churchill wanted to replace coal with oil, but in 1913, the transition had hardly begun. The largest warships carried up to 5,000 tons of coal at full load, but replenished if possible when about 50 percent remained, approximately every week to ten days at economical speeds. Where coaling depots were not available, warships bunkered from colliers of the merchant navy, brought alongside at convenient anchorages.

TOP: *Unidentified mid in the shelter of a gun turret, studying and/or combating seasickness.*
BOTTOM: *Mids cycling in Scotland, properly attired for the activity.*

Apart from the captain and a few key personnel, coaling ship was an all hands evolution. Some laboured with shovels on the dockside or in the hold of a collier to fill bags, which were hoisted by a crane and deposited on the upper deck of the

Artist's impression of the arduous task of feeding the boilers of a coal-powered warship.

receiving ship. From there other men wheeled the coal in barrows to chutes that led to the capacious bunkers along the ship's sides. Inside the bunkers, stokers trimmed the steadily rising piles of coal to keep them level to the very top; the maximum possible tonnage must be embarked. In the last stages the bunkers were carefully watched to ensure the safety of the stokers inside.

The goal was to coal as fast as possible, and competition between ships was intense. A successful coaling required careful planning and organization. Special measures were taken to promote morale and encourage the men to work with enthusiasm. If the ship had a band, it played throughout the evolution. Dress regulation was relaxed to permit men to choose their own outlandish outfits. With the best will in the world, the backbreaking

labour took its toll. By the time the last bag had been gathered in, the ship's company was exhausted. Coal dust covered the upper deck and found its way throughout the ship. Until the vessel was scrubbed clean, however, the men could not wash themselves or their clothes and finally relax, knowing at the same time that in a matter of days it all must be done again. If coaling was discontinued because of bad weather or some other reason, all hands remained in their filthy coaling rig until the job was finally completed. The only redeeming feature was that, by involving the whole crew in a common purpose, *esprit de corps* and a strong ship's spirit were fostered.

When the midshipmen left Canada, the battle to pass Borden's Naval Aid Act was at its height. In May 1913, word arrived that the Act had been rammed through the House of Commons under the threat of closure. It seemed that Canada would indeed pay for the construction of the *Acadia, Quebec*, and *Ontario* for the RN. Whatever the personal feelings of the Canadians, they were left in no doubt about the opinion of their RN mentors. From the British perspective, the dominion had at last come to its senses and done something worthwhile, instead of persisting with Laurier's misguided dream of creating a tinpot navy of its own at some indefinite date in the future.

For two weeks, Canada's stock was high and its cadets regarded with approval. Then came the shattering news that on 29 May the Liberal majority in the Senate defeated the bill. Until enough vacancies arose for Borden to create a Conservative majority in the Upper House, the bill was in limbo and no building funds would be made available to the RN.

Borden had already cancelled Laurier's ship building programme. Thus, for the foreseeable future, the RCN continued to consist of the RNCC and the undermanned, deteriorating *Niobe* and *Rainbow*. At a time of feverish naval competition and growing international tension, Canada in fact had no naval policy. Unfortunately for the cadets, they were the only Canadians available for the venting of RN spleen. The jibes from their British counterparts can be imagined. Even some of the senior officers may not have taken much trouble to conceal their disgust.

These developments were carefully noted by others. When Borden introduced the Naval Aid Bill in the House of Commons, the German naval attaché in London reported:

> It must be assumed that Mr. Borden's bill to place three warships of the newest and largest type at the disposal of the Motherland will be passed in the Canadian Parliament…. It will now have to be reckoned that the three Canadian ships … are a net addition to the (British) programme of construction that was announced in March.

Two weeks later, he reported, "… the British Admiralty has been deprived indefinitely of the windfall of three battleships that they had hoped for."

It cannot have been an easy time for the Canadians, but their training progressed and the routine of port visits continued. Their mementos include references to dances and visits to the theatre. For a complete break there was a period of camping in Cornwall, isolated and wild enough in its own way, but a far cry from their native lakes and forests.

In September of 1913, *Berwick* was ordered to Bermuda, the main base of the RN's North America and West Indies station, with Halifax being a subsidiary port, and became the flagship of the station, which was under the command of the recently promoted Rear-Admiral Sir Christopher

Bermuda was the main base of the Royal Navy's North America and West Indies station. The Canadian mids received a warm welcome.

Cradock. Training cruises continued, but now the ports visited were those of the Caribbean: St Croix, Antigua, Barbados, Dominica. At each one the midshipmen received numerous social invitations from island society, and the ship reciprocated with functions of its own. There was also time enough for the young men to go ashore unofficially, and the Canadians entered into these activities with gusto, as photographs testify. The RN long ago learned that early exposure to the delights of foreign cruises was the best way to convince trainee officers that they had made the right career choice.

In February 1912, Mexican President Madero was shot. General Huerta emerged as his replacement, but a multi-sided civil war ensued. Britain recognized the Huerta government but the United States did not. In the volatile situation, several countries sent warships to Mexican waters to protect their economic interests and, if necessary, to rescue their nationals. *Berwick* spent November and part of December of 1913 on these duties, visiting Vera Cruz and other ports. As the crew relished the prospect of doing something useful, as opposed to the pleasant but boring routines of training, a subtle change of atmosphere occurred.

Tension was high and there was danger. The execution of prisoners of war within a mile of the ship was a daily event. Victor Hatheway's sister reported to the Fredericton *Gleaner* that her brother was slightly wounded in the arm when fired on by a rebel soldier. No evidence has been found that this injury occurred as part of an organized *Berwick* landing operation. Perhaps the young man simply wandered into a dangerous area and found himself in the wrong place at the wrong time.

There were several opportunities to exchange visits with the junior officers of other navies, including the battleship USS *Michigan* and the German

On the outbreak of civil war in Mexico Berwick *was dispatched to protect British interests in the port of Vera Cruz. Rebel prisoners were frequently executed in the main plaza.*

Portraits of William Palmer (left) and John Victor Hatheway (right) in formal dress and wearing midshipman's dirks.

cruiser SMS *Karlsruhe.*[1] Four of the cadets met ships of the latter type again, almost exactly a year later, under very different circumstances.

Having completed their on-board training year, the cadets returned to Canada by early 1914. They should have gone to sea as midshipmen for a further two years before taking their qualifying examination for the rank of sub-lieutenant.

But in the spring of 1914, the only two ships in the RCN were incapable of steaming. As training platforms their value was virtually nil. In all probability, time aboard would not even have counted as sea time. The overall vacuum in Canadian naval policy had brought the careers of these young men to a halt. The politicians hardly concerned themselves with such a minor issue, but for the cadets their future was a matter of serious doubt. Their training, and especially their time in *Berwick* consolidated their commitment to the navy; but if Canada was not ready to support one, they had to consider the possibility of resigning. Their parents must also have questioned their investments. Their sons had received a good, albeit costly, education at the RNCC; but progress in their chosen profession had arrived at a dead end.

From the standpoint of the naval staff, a mass exodus of the first college entry was something to be avoided at all costs. As a temporary expedient,

LEFT: *Midshipmen on quarterdeck of* Berwick.
RIGHT: *Midshipmen observing the complicated seamanship as* Berwick *secures to a buoy.*

the cadets were sent back to the RNCC to take a special course in communications. Guglielmo Marconi had commercialized the use of wireless telegraphy by the early years of the century. Its employment before the *Titanic* disaster and during the subsequent rescue operations highlighted its utility in the maritime environment. All navies hastened to equip their ships with the new technology, which was still rapidly developing. It was well after World War I before voice radio became possible through the use of continuous wave technology. Thus, messages were still transmitted in Morse code, each letter consisting of a set of long or short pulses. If the subject was confidential the sender encrypted the text before transmission. Trained personnel were created from a zero base, and there were many lessons to be learned concerning the strategic and tactical employment of this revolutionary means of communication.

Even as late as 1913, *Berwick's* training syllabus did not include a section on wireless. Apparently,

the RNCC course was designed to rectify this omission, and thus was something more than a way of filling time. The course ended in the late spring of 1914 and the cadets were sent on leave, their naval futures as much in doubt as ever.

At the same time, on the other side of the world, the passenger steamer *Patricia* arrived in China from Germany, carrying replacements for half the crews of the East Asiatic Squadron of the German Navy, being rotated home after their two-year tours in the Far East. This faraway event was not worthy of even a brief report in the Halifax *Chronicle* or the Fredericton *Gleaner.* Even if it had somehow come to their attention, Midshipmen Cann, Hatheway, Palmer and Silver would not have linked it with their own fates.

Germany was a latecomer to the nineteenth century European scramble for colonies. Among the few it acquired were some scattered islands in the Western Pacific ocean and the port of Tsingtao (now Qingdao) on the Shantung peninsula of

Seine Majistats Schiff (SMS) Gneisenau, *sister ship to Admiral von Spee's flagship SMS* Scharnhorst.

China. With typical efficiency and hard work, the port was turned into an Asiatic version of a busy German town. A first-class dockyard was constructed for the support of the East Asiatic Squadron, the only squadron the German navy maintained outside home waters.[2]

At its core were the two modern armoured cruisers *Scharnhorst* and *Gneisenau*, 11,600 ton sister ships, each mounting eight 8.2-inch and six 5.9-inch guns, with a top speed of 22.5 knots and a crew of 765. The squadron also consisted of up-to-date light cruisers *Emden*, *Leipzig*, and *Nurnberg*, and some smaller coastal defense vessels. Most German sailors were conscripts doing three years compulsory service, but the crews of the Asiatic squadron were all long-service men. The squadron was kept at a very high state of efficiency and training. The two armoured cruisers were in fact the gunnery champions of the whole German navy.

Serving as second-in-command or executive officer of *Gneisenau* was Commander Hans Pochammer. He survived World War I, and recorded the saga of the East Asiatic Squadron in his book *Prelude to Jutland*, published in English in 1934. His account provides eyewitness knowledge of the German side of the double tragedy that was to unfold.

Whatever the political differences between Britain and Germany, on a personal level officers of the two navies got on extremely well. In building their navy from virtually nothing, the Germans relied heavily on the example of what had been for more than 100 years the world's largest fleet, and they had a great respect for the RN's power and traditions. For their part, the British sincerely admired the efficiency and professionalism of the young navy that had come so far in such a short time. Unquestionably, their personal relationships with German counterparts were far more cordial

The Japanese battleship Mikasa. *Von Spee had to assume that in the event of war Britain's ally Japan would commit its overwhelming fleet against his squadron.*

than with their French and Russian allies. According to Pochammer, the general opinion of the British officers was that war between the two nations would be madness, and that they ought rather to stand together against the others.

On 12 June 1914, the RN's Far East squadron under Vice-Admiral Sir Martyn Jerram, paid one of its regular goodwill visits to Tsingtao, hosted by Vice-Admiral Graf Maximilian von Spee's squadron. As usual on these occasions, everything possible was done to ensure that the visiting officers and men had an enjoyable time. One year earlier, the German squadron had made a similar visit to Hong Kong. The British had outdone themselves in courtesy to their guests, although Pochammer complained mildly that at a dance aboard *Monmouth*, the British officers practically dragged their guests to the bar, and detained them there in conversation, much restricting their opportunities on the dance floor.

A week after the British visit, von Spee's squadron left Tsingtao on a routine tour of Germany's Far East possessions. The first port of call was Nagasaki, Japan. Having been run down as part of the RN's concentration in home waters, the British force in the Far East was barely a match for the German East Asiatic Squadron. However, British weakness in the theatre was more than offset by the 1902 alliance with Japan. That agreement ensured that in any conflict the entire Japanese navy might be brought into the scales against von Spee. In 1905, the Japanese virtually destroyed the entire Russian fleet, thus becoming the strongest navy in the Far East. It must have been with sober thoughts that the German officers measured the power of the Japanese ships.

By 28 June, von Spee's ships were anchored at the island of Saipan in the Marianas group, purchased from Spain in 1899. The squadron coaled from the commercial colliers that accompanied them, a brutal task in the tropics. Von Spee was a keen amateur naturalist and spent time exploring the island, with one or both of his sons. Meanwhile, his men carried out landing exercises and participated in sports ashore. Most nights the native Polynesians entertained the crews with exhibitions of traditional dancing.

The idyll was terminated by news from Europe, transmitted by the Tsingtao wireless station. On the day von Spee arrived at Saipan, the Austrian Archduke Frederick, heir to the Emperor Franz Josef, made an official visit to the Bosnian town of Sarajevo, then part of the Austro-Hungarian Empire. While driving in an open car, he and his wife were assassinated by the patriot (or terrorist) Gavrilo Princip, acting with the connivance of Serb officers. Independent Serbia had long been an example for the discontented Slavic peoples within the crumbling Empire, which had been seeking an excuse to give the Serbs a lesson.

Fears grew that war would break out between the two, and that it would not be confined to the ever-troublesome Balkans. Russian public opinion might well force the Tsar to come to the aid of his fellow-Slavs. Under the terms of the Triple Alliance this action would oblige Germany to support its ally Austria, in which event France was committed to join Russia. Britain's Entente with France and Russia did not oblige it to go to war in these circumstances, and the Germans sincerely hoped that if war did come Britain would remain neutral.

Artist's impression of the assassination of the heir to the Austro-Hungarian throne, 28 June 1914: the event that ignited the European powder keg.

The assassination coincided with a goodwill visit to Kiel by a British squadron of four battleships and three cruisers, under Rear-Admiral Sir George Warrender. They were guests of the German navy during Kiel Week, one of the world's largest regattas. Officers and men of the squadron were caught up in a whirl of social events, during which numerous friendships with their German counterparts were made or renewed. Beneath the gaiety, many remained soberly aware of the dangers inherent in the international situation. As if to emphasize the underlying tension, Admiral Warrender and other officers were invited to the official opening of the Kiel Canal on 24 June. As the Kaiser arrived for the ceremony, ships of both nations fired a 21-gun salute.

On 28 June, news of the assassination arrived. The German ships hoisted and half-masted the Austrian flag. All entertainments were cancelled. As the British sailed on 30 June, the German admiral signaled, "Pleasant journey" in farewell. Warrender replied, "Friends in the past and friends in future." Sincerely meant, no doubt, but in the circumstances more a hope than a prediction.

Meanwhile, on 7 July, von Spee concentrated his squadron at Truk, where the ships coaled and stored. On 9 July, they received a German Admiralty appreciation predicting that the Triple Alliance would become involved. Two days later they were warned that British neutrality had become problematic. On 19 July, they carried out a night encounter exercise at sea. The next day at Ponape, they began to practice doing without the peacetime comforts to which they were accustomed.

Halfway around the world, on the other side of the international dateline, Canadian newspapers reported on the European crisis with increasing concern. Attention was focused on the forthcoming review of the Royal Navy, a reassuring event in an ever-more-threatening climate. In peacetime the RN was divided into three fleets. The First Fleet consisted of three 8-ship squadrons of the most modern and powerful battleships. It was kept fully manned and in a high state of combat readiness. The Second Fleet, two squadrons of older but still formidable battleships, was manned at the 50 percent level, to be brought to full strength in the event of an emergency by men taken from the training schools. Finally, the Third Fleet was immobilized in dockyard hands, crewed only to the extent necessary to maintain equipment. On

mobilization the ships' companies came from the Royal Naval Reserve of merchant seamen and former regulars, and the Royal Naval Volunteer Reserve of part time sailors.

Once a year the RN conducted manoeuvers in home waters. In 1913, it was decided that in 1914 a test mobilization of the reserve fleets would be carried out instead. By coincidence, the test mobilization took place in mid-July amid increasing international tension over the Serbian crisis. On the morning of 20 July, the entire force passed in review before King George V in the royal yacht, with bands playing and ships' companies cheering from the weather decks. Steaming at 15 knots, it took seven hours for the entire fleet to pass the reviewing vessel, an awesome demonstration of naval might, highly reassuring to friends and hopefully giving pause to potential enemies.

Events were already spinning out of control. Three days after the review, Austria presented an ultimatum to Serbia, so demanding that it seemed impossible that it could be accepted by an independent country. Nevertheless, the Serbs acceded to almost all the conditions. It appeared that war might be averted through intense diplomatic activity. On 25 July, against the advice of his cabinet, Kaiser Wilhelm cut short his annual yachting holiday in Norwegian waters and sailed home, a move that had the unfortunate, if unintended, effect of adding to the tension.

Churchill was also on holiday at his Norfolk cottage, using a neighbour's telephone to keep in touch with the admiralty. On the evening of 26 July, he learned that the Austrians were not content with the Serb reply. Current orders to the fleet required it to disperse after the review, for the purposes of conducting exercises or sending crews on leave. Alarmed, Churchill authorized the First

Sea Lord, Admiral Prince Louis of Battenberg, to keep the First Fleet concentrated at Portland, while the Second Fleet sailed to home ports and remained there in close proximity to its augmentation crews.[3]

In 1914, if Britain declared war Canada was also automatically at war. With two old, undermanned ships, it would be long before the country made a significant contribution at sea. Nevertheless, its trained midshipmen, now enjoying their summer leave, could be put to use somewhere. As they followed the developing international crisis, and the awesome spectacle of the fleet review, the reality of their personal situation hit home. Canada's chaotic naval policy put their futures in jeopardy. They longed for the uncertainty to be removed. War would certainly achieve that, but at what cost?

The commander of the Royal Navy's North America and West Indies station was responsible for defence of British territories in the western Atlantic, including Canada, as well as protection of Britain's seaborne trade, and the elimination of the enemy's ocean commerce. This area included the entire Atlantic Ocean west of longitude 40, from Greenland south to the intersection of the 40 degree meridian with the north coast of Brazil. In July 1914, that man was Rear-Admiral Sir Christopher Cradock, flying his flag in the cruiser HMS *Suffolk*. The sister protected cruisers *Berwick*, *Lancaster*, and *Essex* formed the remainder of his squadron, but, as mobilization proceeded, he also received four Third Fleet armoured cruisers, *Carnarvon*, *Cornwall*, *Cumberland* and *Monmouth*, manned by reservists and not worked up to full combat readiness.

Unable to grow enough food to feed her population, Britain depended on exporting manufactured goods in exchange for grain, meat, tropical

A puckish Winston Churchill observes 1909 German army manoeuvers as a guest of Kaiser Wilhelm. Such courtesy visits ceased when Churchill became First Lord of the Admiralty in 1910.

products and industrial raw materials. The great trade route between Britain and eastern North America was a key artery in this vital circulation, and was vulnerable to attack by enemy surface raiders, either regular warships or commercial vessels fitted out as Armed Merchant Cruisers, AMCs.

As the world drifted toward war, Cradock's information was that two German warships were in his area. One was *Karlsruhe*, which the mids in *Berwick* had met when both vessels monitored the Mexican situation. The second, *Dresden*, another light

Battleships of the British Grand Fleet en route to their war station at Scapa Flow.

cruiser of the same class, just relieved by *Karlsruhe,* was scheduled to return to Germany. The exact location of the vessels was unknown, although both were believed to be in the Caribbean. Cradock was aware of an alleged German plan to conceal guns in the holds of passenger liners on the American run, to be fitted in the event of war. So armed, these swift vessels became AMCs, no match for his ships but a deadly threat on the trade routes. Several German liners were berthed in New York.

Encouraged by the Kaiser, on 26 July, Austria officially rejected the Serbian response to its ultimatum. On 27 July, Cradock in *Suffolk* was at Vera Cruz, where he received a preliminary warning message from the admiralty. The next day Austria declared war on Serbia, and Russia declared war on Austria. The rush to Armageddon gathered momentum as alliance obligations were triggered one by one. During the night of 29 July, accompanied

by supporting cruiser and destroyer squadrons, the 24 British battleships from Portland passed darkened through the Straits of Dover and proceeded to the Grand Fleet's war station at Scapa Flow in the Orkney Islands. On 30 July, the 17 modern battleships of the German High Seas Fleet transited the Kiel Canal from the Baltic to its North Sea harbours. On 1 August, Germany declared war on Russia, and two days later on France.

Apart from Italy, Britain was the only European power not yet engaged. Many in authority hoped to remain neutral. But the German war plan was based on invading France through Belgium, whose neutrality had been guaranteed by all the European powers. When Germany rejected the British ultimatum to withdraw from Belgium, Britain declared war at 11:00 p.m., London time, 4 August, 1914.

Chapter 3
A CUT FLOWER IN A VASE

On 30 July von Spee had received the alert message, "Threatened state of war," the signal for his ships to prepare for action by landing all personal effects, including the many souvenirs the men had acquired. Wooden articles and woodwork stripped from cabins and messes were thrown overboard, bringing into focus the harsh reality of life in a steel box. Von Spee visited each ship in turn. Standing in front of a gun turret, he exhorted his men to make good their oaths to the fatherland. News of the British declaration reached him on 6 August; Pochammer later wrote of the disappointment of officers and men on learning this news, coupled, however, with stern determination to do their duty in all circumstances.

Cradock was searching the Caribbean for *Karlsruhe* when — on 4 August — he received the order, "Commence hostilities against Germany." On 6 August, the enemy ship was sighted, but escaped thanks to superior speed. Cradock was ordered to shift his flag from *Suffolk* to *Good Hope*, which was sailing from Britain to Halifax. Unable to overhaul *Karlsruhe*, he abandoned the chase and proceeded to Halifax for the rendezvous. While passing New York, he received intelligence that *Karlsruhe* was at Puerto Rico and *Dresden* off the mouth of the Amazon. He advised the British Consul General that the Atlantic Ocean north of Trinidad was clear of German warships and transatlantic trade began to flow at its normal volume.

On the day war was declared, the Canadian government placed *Niobe* and *Rainbow* at the disposal of the admiralty. Two days earlier the midshipmen had been ordered to report for duty at the unit nearest their leave addresses.[1] For Malcolm Cann of Yarmouth, John Hatheway of Fredericton and

With war imminent, William Palmer received orders to report for duty while canoeing at the Halifax Waeg-woltic Club.

William Palmer, Arthur Silver, John Grant, G.C. Jones and J.E.W. Oland of Halifax, this meant *Niobe*. Of the rest of their class, four reported at Quebec, four at Ottawa, and three at Esquimalt, for *Rainbow* and the just-purchased submarines *CC-1* and *CC-2*.

The wireless station at Glace Bay was deemed vulnerable to sabotage by local "Austrians," actually ethnic Slavic immigrants from areas then part of the Austrian Empire. A special train carried 54 men from *Niobe* to assist the militia. Midshipmen Palmer and Grant were each placed in charge of a field gun and spent several days on guard duties until the vital point was considered secure. For the first time they carried loaded pistols; a new reality was setting in.

Suffolk arrived at Halifax the evening of Thursday, 13 August. The ship coaled throughout the night, assisted by the officers and men of the 63rd Rifles, a local militia unit. Thirsting for action, and with *Niobe* jetty-bound, the midshipmen volunteered to join *Suffolk*. They went aboard shortly before it sailed on the Friday afternoon, a classic "pier head jump." Their departure was newsworthy. The Saturday edition of the Halifax *Herald* headlined: "Brave Halifax Lads Eager to Strike for Canada and the Empire." Almost as though it was a pleasure cruise, the article noted, "Halifax will look forward to their visits to this port throughout the duration of the war." It was not long before such peacetime sentiments vanished in the carnage.

On Saturday, 15 August, *Good Hope* arrived and, according to the *Herald*, sailed on the same day, only half coaled. Something had gone wrong because *Suffolk* and *Good Hope* should have met in Halifax for Cradock's change of flagship. Apparently, after coaling, *Suffolk* could not wait even for one day, forcing *Good Hope* to coal hurriedly and hasten to follow.

At this time, or earlier, it was discovered that *Good Hope* was four short of the established complement of midshipmen.[2] The shortfall was made up from the Canadian mids on board *Suffolk*. All seven would have volunteered. According to John Grant, who was one of them, Cradock personally asked for William Palmer, first in his graduating class, and Arthur Silver, who had been the senior Cadet Captain.[3] The other two were chosen by lot; chance dictated that Malcolm Cann's and Victor Hatheway's names were drawn. Transfer to a larger and more powerful vessel, and a flagship at that, was a plum assignment. The three not selected would be bitterly disappointed. But within six weeks their much-envied comrades were dead.

The four appointments to *Good Hope* were dated 17 August 1914. The two ships met at sea, and Cradock, his dog, his small staff and the four midshipmen were transferred by boat. In the course of the evolution, an irreplaceable Chinese vase, the admiral's only valuable possession, was accidentally broken. Captain Franklin of *Suffolk* and a few of his officers changed places with Captain Yelverton and some officers of *Good Hope*. Cradock thus continued to work with a flag captain he had come to know and trust.

The four mids found themselves in their third

operate the winches during this evolution. Hoisting the sacks of coal from the collier's hold and depositing them on the deck of the cruiser was a task requiring significant skill and concentration; poor winch operation guaranteed a poor coaling.

In *Whispers from the Fleet*, Cradock argued in a passage that showed the supreme self-confidence of the pre-World War I Royal Navy:

HMS Good Hope, *Halifax, 15 August 1914. Two days later she became Admiral Cradock's flagship and the four mids transferred to her at sea.*

ship in just two weeks, *Niobe*, *Suffolk*, and now *Good Hope*. Life on board was a far cry from peacetime conditions. They were warned not to bring unnecessary items of clothing or personal effects. Like all ships at the outbreak of war, *Good Hope* was stripped of woodwork and wooden furniture; nothing remained to soften the impact of the steel box in which they were enclosed.

Under Cradock's command, *Swiftsure* had set the British coaling record of 365 tons per hour. Efficient coaling remained a fixation, because unnecessary time taken in this evolution seriously affected operations. In keeping with his emphasis on coaling, Cradock insisted that midshipmen

Again I wonder! — Do officers and men in a bad coaling unenterprizing ship, ever realize the fact that making continuous heavy weather over this unavoidable and important evolution of coaling, may one day spell for them the fateful words 'too late'; at a time when the smoke of the enemies' burning vessels will be all that speaks to them of the great general action which they were destined never to see. — To share in which, as a birthright, they have long toiled and slaved in the past; and now in the bitter present, would gladly give their disappointed lives not to have missed.

HMS Good Hope. *Note the forward 9.2-inch gun, and the main deck 6-inch casemates near the waterline.*

An entire chapter of Cradock's book *Whispers from the Fleet* was devoted to advice for junior officers. It begins with the words "Obedience is the soul of the navy; he who has not learned to obey, is wanting in the first essential of command" and goes on to say, "A midshipman's boat and gun should be to him his prime interest and delight." *Whispers* was published only five years earlier. No doubt those mids who had not already read it seized the first opportunity to do so, now that they found themselves in Cradock's flagship.

Armoured flagship though it was, and proud as the mids were to be aboard, it was not long before they realized that much was amiss with *Good Hope*. On paper it was relatively modern, having been built in 1902, being at that time the fastest cruiser in the RN. But 12 years later it had fallen behind the dizzy pace of technical improvement. Propelled by reciprocating engines, rather than the more reliable turbines, steam for the engines was generated by coal. At full load the ship carried 5,000 tons for 43 boilers, consuming 10 tons per hour at normal cruising speed, rising to nearly 25 tons at full speed. The need to coal at frequent intervals was a major strategic limitation when no British base was nearby. Finally, like all coal-driven ships, clouds of dark smoke belched from each of the four funnels, a bane to cleanliness and an ever-present early warning to an enemy vessel.

In 1908, *Good Hope* was fitted with a rudimentary fire control system, but the armament was woefully out of date, reflecting the era when battles were fought at relatively close ranges by ships armed with the largest possible number of guns of heavy and medium calibre. The main armament consisted of only two 9.2 inch guns in single turrets forward and aft, with a maximum range of 12,500 yards. Sixteen 6-inch guns formed a powerful secondary battery. They were single mountings, each in a rotating casemate protruding from the upper or the main deck. When the gun ports were open, the main deck casemates might be flooded in heavy seas, and aiming was always difficult because of the low height of eye. Lord Fisher commented, "... the guns on the main deck are practically useless. We know this from experience. Half the time they cannot see the target for want of view, and the other half they are flooded out by the sea." Their maximum range was 11,200 yards, which meant a 1,300 yard gap within which the 9.2-inch, but not the 6-inch could reach the target.

Good Hope was a Third Fleet ship, with reservists forming a very high proportion of the crew. After participating in the July fleet review, the augmentation crew had either remained aboard or been recalled as war became increasingly probable. Beyond preparing for hostilities, however, there was little or no time for workups before it was ordered to the North America station. Only four rounds of practice ammunition had been issued, far too few for a raw crew that had yet to learn to work as a team. Only one firing practice was conducted en route to Halifax. The few mids already on board were merchant navy officer apprentices enrolled in the Royal Naval Reserve. While accustomed to life at sea, as compared with the four Canadian mids, they lacked academic and military qualifications. Thus, the Canadians were probably assigned more challenging responsibilities than would have been the case in a ship manned by regulars. In contrast with *Berwick*, they filled positions in the ship's establishment, rather than being supernumerary trainees. It is not possible to link each individual with particular duties, but the general nature of their employment can be guessed with reasonable certainty. They would be addressed as "mid," the pejorative "snotty" no longer appropriate. There might be more "doggy" duties. Their recent special communications course no doubt proved very useful in a ship where that expertise was rare. At sea, they would have done duty as midshipman of the watch, and one of them may have had this position on the bridge at action stations. In *Berwick*, they had qualified to take charge of a 6-inch gun crew.

John Victor Hatheway with Admiral Cradock's dog.

One or more of them may have assumed this role in *Good Hope*. Certainly, at least one was part of the ship's gunnery fire control team, spotting the fall of shot or calculating range and bearing rates.

Good Hope's problems were no secret. As it left Portsmouth for Halifax, a Salvation Army band is said to have played, "Nearer My God to Thee," an ill-omened, but sadly appropriate choice.

In mid-August 1914, Cradock in *Good Hope* was in the North Atlantic, off New York. Von Spee and his East Asiatic squadron were in the Pacific, at Eniwetok in the Marshall Islands, coaling as usual. In different oceans, with North and South America between them, essentially on opposite sides of the world, both commanders had serious decisions to make and many things to consider; but at this point neither had any reason to be concerned with the other's force or location.

Rear-Admiral Sir Christopher George Francis Maurice Cradock, KCVO, CB, RN, was 52 years old, 39 of which he had spent in the Royal Navy. As a junior officer he served in the Royal Yacht. He distinguished himself in two land campaigns. The first was at the capture of the fort of Tokar in 1891, as an aide-de-camp in an Anglo-Egyptian expedition to the Sudan. The second was in 1900, when he commanded *Alacrity*, the yacht of the commander-in-chief of the China station. Peasants organized as the Society of Harmonious Fists, better known as Boxers, rebelled against the Chinese government and besieged the foreign legations in Peking. Cradock was with a multinational force of sailors and marines under the British Admiral Seymour, fighting its way slowly toward the capital. On one occasion the column was held up by rebel snipers in a narrow pass, until Cradock and the future Admiral Beatty mounted their horses and in full view led the troops forward, apparently oblivious to the bullets whizzing around them. A complex of forts at Taku formed a major barrier to the advance.

Rear-Admiral Sir Christopher Cradock.

Here Cradock led a combined British, Japanese, and German force in an assault against heavy fire. A Japanese officer was the first over the parapet, with Cradock just behind him; the Japanese was immediately killed, but Cradock rallied the men and drove the Boxers from their defences. For this exploit the German government awarded him the Order of the Crown, with Swords.[4] At one time, he commanded the armoured cruiser *Leviathan*, a sister ship to *Good Hope*. In 1908, he was captain of the pre-dreadnought battleship *Swiftsure* in the Channel Fleet, which, ironically in light of future events, had originally been built for the Chilean navy. Admiral Fisher, the First Sea Lord, called Cradock "one of our very best officers."

He was promoted to Rear-Admiral in 1910. In 1912, the liner *Delhi* wrecked on the coast of Morocco and Cradock organized the rescue of the survivors, including the Princess Royal and her family. For this service was awarded the KCVO. He assumed command of the North America and West Indies Station in 1913.

He wrote three books, *Sporting Notes in the Far East* (1889), *Wrinkles in Seamanship* (1894), and *Whispers from the Fleet* (1907). Their titles illustrate his range of interests. He was supposed to have said that he wished to die either in a fox hunting accident or in a naval action. Always immaculately dressed, he remained a bachelor throughout his life.

It would be hard to describe *Whispers* as anything but a dry, largely unorganized aggregation of useful and useless tips. Yet, in the middle of it, seemingly out of nowhere, Cradock wrote the following uncannily prescient passage:

> *A heaving unsettled sea, and away over to the western horizon an angry yellow sun is setting clearly below a forbidding bank of the blackest of wind-charged clouds. In the centre of the picture lies an immense solitary cruiser*

with a flag — 'tis the cruiser recall at her mast-head blowing out broad and clear from the first rude kiss given by the rising breeze. Then away, from half the points of the compass, are seen the swift ships of a cruiser squadron all drawing in to join their flagship: — some are close, others far distant and hull down, with nothing but their fitful smoke against the fast-fading lighted sky to mark their whereabouts; but like wild ducks at evening flighting home to some well-known spot, so are they, with one desire, hurry-ing back at the behest of their mother ship to gather round her for the night.

At a time when many deemed the *matériel* side to be all-important, Cradock saw the navy not merely as a collection of ships, but as a community of men united by a higher purpose.

Vice-Admiral Graf (Count) Maximilian von Spee was one year older than Cradock. He had entered the navy at the age of 16. He came from a

Vice-Admiral Graf Maximilian von Spee.

family of Catholic nobility domiciled in the Rhine-land and was happily married. As a junior officer, he served in German West Africa and later com-manded that station, but was invalided home with a fever that left him subject to rheumatic attacks for the rest of his life. He held staff appointments in the key field of mine warfare development and became a gunnery expert. He commanded the minelayer *Pelikan* and the cruiser *Hela*. He was

Chief of Staff of the North Sea Fleet in 1908, while captain of the pre-dreadnought battleship *Wittles-bach*. He was promoted to Rear-Admiral in 1910, as second in command of the High Seas Fleet's scout-ing force. In 1912, he assumed command of the East Asiatic Squadron at Tsingtao, with the rank of Vice-Admiral.

He was tall and strongly built, with an aggressive but at the same time serene and fatalistic person-ality. He was a keen bridge player and an active amateur naturalist, who never missed an opportunity to pursue his hobby in tropical harbours. His sons Otto and Heinrich were lieutenants in his squad-ron, serving in *Nurnberg* and *Gneisenau*.

Immediately after the war, the creator of the Ger-man Navy, Grand-Admiral von Tirpitz, published his memoirs. He mentions that shortly before the war von Spee and Cradock met and became friends. Quite possibly this meeting occurred during a goodwill visit when both of-ficers were commanding old battleships, *Wittlesbach* and *Swiftsure*. In fact, they might have become acquainted some years ear-lier. Von Spee was chief of staff to Prince Henry of Prussia, who commanded the German forces participating in the Boxer rebellion during which Cradock had so distinguished himself. However it came about, their friendship was but another ex-ample of the excellent pre-war personal relations between officers of the two navies.

Both commanders came of wealthy and distinguished families, and both were highly professional and full of fighting spirit. In a way, they were characteristic of the senior officers their respective services tended to produce: Cradock the consummate and action-oriented seaman, von Spee the intellectual planner and weapons expert.

It was von Spee who faced the most difficult decisions: how was his powerful force to be employed now that war had commenced? The German mission was to inflict economic injury consistent with international law, to prevent or delay the transport of enemy troops, while forcing the allies to divert resources to search for them. They would fight only if enemy forces interfered with that mission. As Pochammer wrote with impressive clarity:

> *It was the enemy's business to seek out and destroy us; ours to avoid him, to lead him astray and threaten to be perpetually turning up, to engage the attention of as many of his ships as possible, in order to relieve the home force to that extent, and, despite all obstacles to reach the important trade routes.*

Grand–Admiral Alfred Friedrich von Tirpitz, creator of the modern German navy.

Unfortunately for the British, until too late, they did not express their own aims so clearly.

Very sensibly, the German naval war staff left the decision entirely to the admiral himself. None of von Spee's strategic alternatives were attractive. Japanese and British forces in Far East waters would overwhelm him if he defended Tsingtao and other German possessions. Troop convoys from India, Australia and New Zealand to France were high value targets, but well escorted by forces superior to his own. In the end, the least bad option was to operate against undefended allied trade on the west coast of South America, where no British ships were stationed. In Chile, he had numerous sources of intelligence and opportunities to charter colliers to replenish his vital coal supplies. With its large German immigrant population, he could count on a good reception at the port of Valparaiso.

In the background loomed the scarcely acknowledged possibility of passing through the Straits of Magellan to emerge on the South Atlantic trade routes, and even to attempt against all odds to return to Germany, a feat that involved eluding or fighting through the entire British Grand Fleet blocking both entrances to the North Sea. Success was so unlikely that Churchill saw von Spee's powerful but isolated squadron as "… a cut flower in a vase, fair to see but bound to die." In his heart the German admiral would probably have agreed.

Cradock decided that, whether armed or not, the German passenger liners would not sail from New York, and also that *Karlsruhe* and *Dresden*, operating independently, were generally moving in a southerly direction. Thus, the enemy threat in the North Atlantic was no longer serious. On the other hand, it seemed likely to increase in South American waters, where the trade route to the United Kingdom was almost as important as that from North America.

The light cruiser HMS Glasgow, *the fastest and best-manned ship in Cradock's squadron.*

The admiralty shared Cradock's opinion and set up a South American squadron under his command. In peacetime the RN did not have a South American Station, but HMS *Glasgow*, under Captain John Luce, had showed the flag and collected intelligence in the area well before the war began. *Glasgow* was a fast modern light cruiser with two 6-inch and ten 4-inch guns, and the only ship under Cradock's command with a full regular force crew. Based at the Falkland Islands, one of its roles was to identify and chart safe anchorages outside the coastal states' three mile limits. If war came, British ships could use them to replenish their bunkers from colliers without breaking international rules of neutrality.

Aboard *Glasgow* was Paymaster Lieutenant Lloyd Hirst. He was Captain Luce's intelligence officer. His normal duties, as what is now called a logistics officer, required him to make arrangements for supplies and fuel by going ashore in foreign ports. This provided cover for his real job of visiting British consuls to gather intelligence on German activities, especially the chartering and movements of colliers and supply vessels. After Cradock's appointment, Hirst became the intelligence officer for the whole squadron, but temporarily remained in *Glasgow* instead of joining *Good Hope*. His book *Coronel and After*, published in 1934, the same year as Pochammer's *Prelude to Jutland*, provides a similar first-person account from the British perspective.

In addition to *Good Hope*, Cradock was given *Glasgow*, the protected cruiser *Monmouth*, and the armed merchant cruiser *Otranto*. *Monmouth* was lightly armoured, had an introductory fire control system, and 14 6-inch guns. Many were in casemates on the main deck, subject to the same weather and aiming deficiencies as the main deck 6-inch guns in the flagship. Hirst recorded in his diary, "She is only half equipped and is not in a condition to come 6000 miles from any dockyard as she is only kept going by superhuman efforts." The AMC *Otranto* was a passenger liner taken

The protected cruiser HMS Monmouth, *same class as* Berwick, *obsolescent and in poor repair.*

up from trade and fitted with four 4.7-inch guns. AMCs were normally employed defending merchant vessels against enemy AMCs, or capturing enemy merchant ships. In Cradock's squadron, *Otranto's* main role was to form part of a search line with the other ships. *Otranto's* Royal Naval Reserve merchant naval crew steamed and navigated the vessel as before, with one Royal Navy regular officer and gun crews posted aboard to fight the ship if necessary.

Cradock's squadron continued to search for the elusive *Karlsruhe* and *Dresden* in Brazilian waters. His ships operated between the coaling anchorages that *Glasgow* identified, one on English Bank, near the mouth of the River Plate, and the other at the Abrolhos Rocks off the north-east coast of Brazil. He was unaware that *Dresden* was already en route to the Pacific via Cape Horn, or that *Karlsruhe* was still in the Caribbean.[5] *(See map page 61)*

For lack of a better alternative, von Spee decided to proceed to the west coast of South America, with a focus on Valparaiso. In the absence of intelligence, the admiralty suspected that this was his most probable course of action. On 14 September, they so signalled to Cradock and directed him to concentrate a force strong enough to meet the Germans, to be based at the Falkland Islands, where there was a coaling station. He was advised that the old battleship *Canopus* and the powerful armoured cruiser *Defence* were on their way to reinforce him. The signal ended, "Until *Defence* arrives keep *Canopus* and *Monmouth* with flagship. As soon as you have superior force search Magellan Straits, being ready to return and cover Plate, or search north as far as Valparaiso. Destroy German cruisers."

Thus, the port of Valparaiso came to figure in the plans of both admirals: for von Spee a firm destination, for Cradock a boundary to a potential reconnaissance by part of his force. By mid-September, von Spee was at Apia in Samoa, nearly 10,300 kilometers from Valparaiso; Cradock, in *Good Hope*, was off the River Plate, about 4,800 km (3,000 miles) from the same place, a separation of 15,100 km (9,400 miles) or nearly 8,200 nautical miles. When the four Canadians joined *Good Hope* between Halifax and New York one month earlier, von Spee was in the Marshall Islands. The distance between the squadrons via Cape Horn was then more than 28,000 km (17,000 miles). Neither admiral was focused on the other, but in less than a month circumstances had conspired to bring them 13,000 km (8,000 miles) nearer to contact.

In early October, Victor Hatheway's sister, Mrs. George Howie, received a letter from her brother, probably written from the River Plate. To conceal the location of the ship, it was postmarked Liverpool, England; thus, it crossed the Atlantic twice. It must therefore have been written about mid-September or earlier. In the last line, Victor wrote: "We are hot on the trail of the enemy ships," that is *Dresden* and *Karlsruhe*. His morale was high and

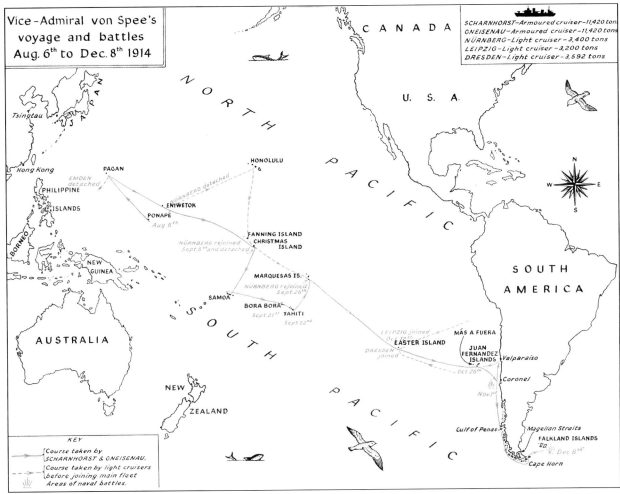

The voyage of the East Asiatic Squadron to victory at Coronel and disaster at the Falkland Islands.

von Spee's squadron had yet to become the object of Cradock's strategy.

William Palmer also expected "to finish the business soon," but complained of the monotonous routine. "You would think it was very exciting, but in reality it is damned slow. We are so damned sick of it we would give anything to see the enemy." In a transparent attempt to acquaint his family with his whereabouts, against regulations, he remarked "Phew, but it's hot here."

The admiralty's message of 14 September can be criticized on many grounds, including the ambiguity of the tasks assigned to Cradock. If he searched as far north as Valparaiso, with a force superior to von Spee's, the latter might elude him, pass through the Straits from west to east, and emerge

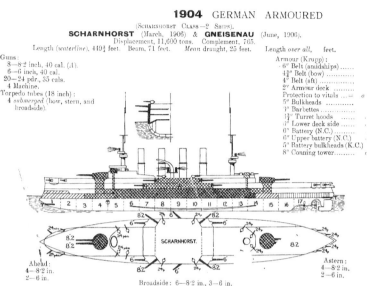

1904 GERMAN ARMOURED

(Scharnhorst Class—2 Ships).

SCHARNHORST (March, 1906) & **GNEISENAU** (June, 1906).

Displacement, 11,600 tons. Complement, 765.

Length (waterline), 449¾ feet. Beam, 71 feet. Mean draught, 25 feet. Length over all, feet.

Guns :
8—8·2 inch, 40 cal. (A).
6—6 inch, 40 cal.
20—24 pdr., 35 cals.
4 Machine.
Torpedo tubes (18 inch) :
4 submerged (bow, stern, and broadside).

Armour (Krupp) :
6″ Belt (amidships) ......
4¾″ Belt (bow) ....
4″ Belt (aft) ....
2″ Armour deck ....
Protection to vitals ... *a*
5″ Bulkheads ....
3″ Barbettes ....
1¾″ Turret hoods ......
3″ Lower deck side ......
6″ Battery (N.C.) ......
6″ Upper battery (N.C.)
5″ Battery bulkheads (K.C.)
8″ Conning tower......... *c*

Machinery : 2 sets vertical inverted triple expansion. 3 cylinder : one set, central, 4 cylinder. 3 screws. Boilers : 18 Schulz Thornycroft. Designed H.P. 26,000 = 22·5 kts. Coal : *normal* 800 tons ; *maximum* 2000 tons (also 200 tons oil).

Armour Notes.—

Gunnery Notes.—Hoists, electric and hand (one serving two or three guns). Masthead fire controls fitted 1912.

Torpedo Notes.—6 searchlights. Electrical installation at 115 volts. Two turbo generators each 4000 r.p.m.—load, 850 amperes.

Engineering Notes.—Full speed 120 revs. 95 = 20·5 kts. *about.* The three engine rooms separated by solid bulkheads. Boiler rooms ditto.

Name.	Builders.	Machinery.	Laid down.	Completed.	Refit.	Trials, full power.		Boilers.	Best recent speed.
Gneisenau	Weser, Bremen.		1904	1907			= 24·8	S. Th'nyc'ft.	24·8
Scharnhorst	Blohm & Voss, Hamburg.		1905	1907		18,032 = 20·7	27,759 = 22·7	S. Th'nyc'ft.	21

General Notes.—Scharnhorst grounded badly in 1909 and since then has never been able to steam as well as before. These carry two 200 h.p. 48 feet motor launches (16 kts.), 1—8 kt. motor barge, 2 steam boats.

German armoured cruiser specifications, Janes Fighting Ships, 1914 edition.

on the trade routes with Cradock far behind. The message also failed to define what constituted a superior force. *Canopus* was a pre-dreadnought battleship, built in 1900, with a top speed of only 16 knots and a typical mixed, outdated armament of four 12-inch and 12 6-inch guns. Largely manned by reservists, the gun turret officers had never been in a turret before the war, and there was no opportunity for practice shoots. However, *Canopus* had strong armour protection against the large calibre shells of enemy battleships and was, therefore, relatively invulnerable to the lighter armament of the German cruisers. Nevertheless, one interpretation of the message was that, even with the old battleship in company, Cradock would not have superior force until *Defence* arrived.

There was much to consider and not only by the admiral. Action with a light cruiser would not have been unwelcome, and even looked forward to by the mids and the whole ship's company. Now, however, the opponent might well be von Spee's crack squadron. One can imagine the crew frequently consulting *Jane's Fighting Ships* and the heated discussions of relative fighting values in wardroom, gunroom, and mess decks. Halifax must suddenly have seemed much further away.

Von Spee detached *Nurnberg* to call at Honolulu to deliver and collect mail and to initiate arrangements to supply his squadron when it reached South America. *Nurnberg* was previously stationed in Mexican waters and would not necessarily be perceived as operating with the East Asiatic Squadron.

Von Spee intended to make for South America, but even with advance planning it would take time for German representatives to charter colliers to replenish his bunkers. In the meantime he decided to damage allied interests in the central Pacific. At the beginning of the war, an expedition from New Zealand captured Apia, the capital of German Samoa. Von Spee lacked the resources to recapture it, but hoped that a surprise arrival would trap some reinforcement shipping. At dawn on 14 September, his squadron appeared off the harbour. There was nothing there, so he sailed away. When last seen by the New Zealanders, he was steering to the northwest, in the opposite direction to South America. This information was passed to the admiralty, which was completely fooled by von Spee's ruse and wrongly deduced that his objective was Fiji or even New Zealand.

Two days later, Cradock was informed that in view of this development his cruisers need no longer be concentrated. Two of them, plus *Otranto*, should watch the Magellan Straits and attack German trade off the Chilean coast. At the same time, the admiralty cancelled the order for *Defence* to join Cradock, but failed to inform him. Search for the elusive *Dresden* continued. *Glasgow* and *Monmouth* proceeded to Valparaiso, where Lieutenant Hirst bought up all the available Chilean charts, hoping that if the Germans did arrive they would not possess any of their own. On the way south, the two cruisers searched every mousehole on the intricate coast and concluded, correctly, that *Dresden* was already far to the north.

During and after the war, there was much criticism of admiralty staff work in 1914 and 1915. Until 1912, there had never been an operational staff, nor had any special training been carried out. In the days of sail it took weeks or months for information to travel between London and the RN's overseas stations. Therefore, the Admiralty Board confined itself to giving broad instructions to local commanders, trusting to the initiative and judgment of the man on the spot to achieve the desired results.

This approach changed with the advent of wireless and intercontinental undersea cables, with communication time measured in days if not hours. The admiralty could keep up with an overall strategic situation that could change at a pace never before experienced. For a time, senior officers continued to believe that they could personally absorb the vastly increased flow of information and make effective operational decisions. As late as 1909, the naval war plan was carried in the head of the First Sea Lord.

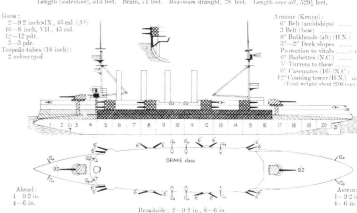

Good Hope *specifications, Janes Fighting Ships, 1914 edition.*

Under the new First Lord, Winston Churchill, a naval staff was imposed upon the admirals, and those who could not adapt were forced to resign.

Unfortunately, now that rapid communications were possible, the temptation to overmanage distant events was tempting. The newly formed staff was inexperienced, incompetent, and over-centralized. Even minor decisions in every theatre of war were passed to the Chief of Staff, Vice-Admiral Sir Frederick Doveton Sturdee, who was a poor delegator. He and the First Sea Lord, Prince Louis of

SMS Dresden. *Von Spee's fastest ship and the last survivor of the East Asiatic Squadron.*

King George V, whom he had known when the latter served in the navy: "I have a feeling that the two heavy cruisers from China are making for the Straits of Magellan and am just off there to search and see." En route he met the British liner *Ortega*, whose captain reported that he was chased by *Dresden* on the south-west coast of South America, but escaped at high speed through an uncharted channel. Cradock unsuccessfully searched the Magellan Straits for *Dresden* before proceeding to the Falkland Islands to coal. *Glasgow, Monmouth* and *Otranto* were ordered to return to the west coast to search as far north as Valparaiso. *Good Hope* remained as a back up in case *Dresden* doubled back. *Glasgow's* Captain Luce tried to convince Cradock to send *Glasgow* without the two slower ships, but the admiral rejected his advice outright.

The Falkland Islands consist of 4,700 square miles of barren, wind-swept sheep pasture. Spring was just beginning in the southern hemisphere, but the prevailing weather was overcast and damp, with constant strong winds for which the region is notorious. In 1914, there were around 2,000 inhabitants. More than half lived in the capital, Port Stanley, situated on the eastern and larger of the two main islands. It had a deep enclosed harbour, used mainly for the export of wool and mutton and the import of food and other necessities. It was of strategic importance because of large coal stocks and a wireless station, both vital to the Royal Navy.

There was no British garrison, but under the leadership of the governor, an ill-armed but enthusiastic local militia was called out, trenches dug, and plans made for the defence of Port Stanley against a raiding force. Cradock was impressed and wrote to the governor, "I shall not fail to let them know at home officially what I have seen and think

Battenberg, were worked almost to death. To make matters worse, the combative and over-confident Churchill intervened at the operational level to an unprecedented extent, on occasion originating orders without consulting the First Sea Lord in advance.

Arguably, systemic deficiencies at the centre of the RN's mighty machine largely determined the fate of the four Canadian midshipmen and the nearly 2,500 men of Cradock's squadron.

On 20 September, *Good Hope* sailed south from the River Plate. Before leaving, Cradock wrote to of your gallant precautions and plan for upholding our honor against attack by von Spee. Would that all our dependencies were the same." Since the last major port Cradock visited before the Falklands was Halifax, where he found a broken-down cruiser and a bankrupt naval policy, there is little doubt that he included Canada among the dependencies that were falling short. At the same time, what is known about Cradock's character suggests that he would not let his feelings about their country's naval policy affect his dealings with the Canadian midshipmen, the only immediate assistance the RCN was able to give him.

Insignificant outpost that it was, Port Stanley provided the first opportunity for rest and relaxation that the Canadian mids and the crew of *Good Hope* enjoyed since leaving Halifax more than a month earlier. The break was needed because conditions on board were not good. Concert parties and deck hockey provided some relief from the strain of steaming in two watches, but the stresses accumulated. Almost everyone on board suffered from prickly heat, and it had proved impossible to eradicate an infestation of cockroaches. There was no air conditioning and the ship's modest refrigeration capability had broken down. The potatoes had spoiled, and the bread baked on board from mouldy flour was almost too sour to eat. Most meals consisted of corned beef and boiled rice. About this time Cradock put the squadron on half rations.[6]

Private mail to and from ships at sea was routed to the United Kingdom with official correspondence. It arrived unpredictably and after long delays. Many weeks of letters awaited the ship in Port Stanley, but none from Canada. No doubt the disappointed midshipmen nevertheless wrote home. Palmer at last managed to convey his location by sending a postcard through

William Palmer's Port Stanley postcard to his family, sent through the civilian mail. He thus managed to convey his whereabouts in contravention of censorship rules.

the civilian postal system, bearing a Falklands stamp and with a photo of Port Stanley.

For many, Stanley's most welcome amenity was the unusually strong beer available at the Falkland Arms or the Rose and Crown. On board, the midshipmen were allowed a wine bill of ten shillings a month; at three or four pennies a glass this amounted to one drink per day. No doubt the young men indulged in a few glasses of beer as they explored the limited attractions of the town's small commercial district or tramped the surrounding moors.

The sudden availability of alcohol proved too much for the *Good Hope's* sailors, badly fed and too long under strain. Many got horribly drunk. On the first day of leave, 20 of them fell into the harbour at the boat landing. Pity the unfortunate mids in charge of the liberty boats! One stoker, jailed after a brawl, became the *Good Hope's* sole survivor, when the ship sailed without him. Captain

Leipzig *leaving Tsingtao before the war, for duty on the west coast of Mexico. She later rejoined von Spee, after a near encounter with HMCS* Rainbow *off San Francisco.*

Francklin published an order reminding the ship's company that it was an offence to render oneself unfit for duty; thereafter, there was little trouble.

These few days ashore temporarily masked, but did not dispel, the concerns that were now a feature of daily life. Every officer and man knew that the distance between the ship and von Spee's squadron was steadily decreasing. Whether or not the two forces met depended on decisions made by the admiralty and by their commander, decisions they could not influence, but must simply accept and do their duty.

Meanwhile von Spee bombarded Papeete, capital of the French colony of Tahiti, destroying a gunboat and causing the governor to burn the coal stocks. His squadron then proceeded to the Marquesas Islands, where it anchored from 26 September to 4 October, coaling and replenishing food supplies. Von Spee's operators unexpectedly established wireless contact with *Dresden* at a range of 3,000 miles. Though not under his command, now that he was aware she was in the Pacific, von Spee ordered the ship to join him. Before the war, the light cruiser *Leipzig* was detached from his squadron to look after German interests on the west coast of Mexico; it, too, was ordered to rejoin.[7]

The East Asiatic Squadron's position at this time was a mystery to the British, but on 4 October, the radio station at Suva intercepted von Spee's wireless message ordering *Leipzig* and *Dresden* to meet him at Easter Island. Perhaps because *Dresden* did not hold crypto material for the Pacific station this message was transmitted in the clear. The admiralty realized that it had been deceived by von Spee's north-westerly course on leaving Apia, and that he was definitely heading east for South America, not south-west for Fiji or New Zealand.

Cradock always considered this to be von Spee's most probable course of action, so was not surprised to receive an admiralty message on 5 October, directing him to send *Canopus* to the west coast. If Cradock chose to accompany, *Monmouth* was to return to the Falklands as backstop. In his reply, Cradock suggested that von Spee would soon have three light cruisers with the armoured cruisers *Scharnhorst* and *Gneisenau*, a correct deduction. He asked when *Defence* would join him and was belatedly informed that it was not assigned to his command. Instead, the admiralty established a new squadron, including *Defence,* to be based off the River Plate, in case von Spee eluded Cradock and appeared in the Atlantic.

Chapter 4
AT THE GOING DOWN OF THE SUN

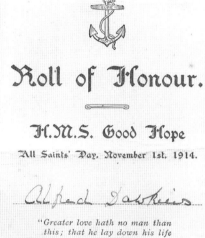

Without *Defence*, Cradock's cruiser squadron remained inferior to von Spee's, unless *Canopus*, with its 12-inch guns, could tip the balance. There were mixed opinions. On the German side, Pochammer was sure that they could "brush the old tub aside," but von Spee thought "… against the latter [*Canopus*] we can hardly do anything." Except in very unusual circumstances, he of course had the option of using his speed to stay well clear of the old battleship.[1]

Canopus joined Cradock at Port Stanley on 22 October, two days later than expected. Captain Grant signalled that five days were needed to repair condensers, and even then maximum speed would be only 12 knots, not the expected 16. Cradock's dilemma was obvious: with *Canopus* in company, he could engage von Spee with some hope of success or, at least, of survival. But with the old

battleship, his squadron was restricted to its best speed, too slow to force an action if von Spee chose to avoid one.

On 18 October, Cradock reported, "I fear that strategically the speed of my squadron cannot exceed 12 knots owing to *Canopus*, but trust circumstances will enable me to force an action." This sentence was open to two interpretations. One, accepted by Churchill and the admiralty, was that Cradock would remain with the slow *Canopus*, even if that meant that he could not bring von Spee to action. The other, probably intended by Cradock, was that if necessary he would dispense with the support of *Canopus* in order to force von Spee to fight.

As the aide to the governor of the Falklands remembered it:

Officers of Good Hope. *Front row, Silver, third from left; Cann, fourth from left; Palmer, second from right. Hatheway not present, probably on duty.*

The admiral was a very brave old man: he knew he was going to almost certain death in fighting these new and powerful ships and it seemed to be quite all right as far as he was concerned.... He knew what he was up against and asked for a fast cruiser with big guns to be added to his squadron for he had nothing very powerful and nothing very fast, but the Admiralty said he'd have to do without. So *old Cradock said "all right; we'll do without" and he slipped quietly off early one morning and left Canopus to look after the colliers and picked up Glasgow and Monmouth and set off to look for those crack Germans.*

Before leaving Port Stanley, Cradock buried his decorations in the garden of the governor's residence and left a sealed package to be sent to his friend Admiral Meux in the event of his death.

The crew of *Good Hope* were not privy to their admiral's thoughts or private conversations, but his signal traffic with the admiralty was known at least to some. Many, including the four Canadians, must have felt relief at the arrival of *Canopus* at Port Stanley; perhaps the odds against them were not so bad after all. Their hearts must have sunk when the reinforcement was left behind, with little hope of catching up.

All knew that, in deciding his own fate, Cradock was also deciding theirs. The officers were also aware that Admiral Cradock and Captain Francklin had become estranged and rarely spoke except on duty. Franklin had been an instructor at the War College and would have offered useful advice had they remained on good terms, but the admiral tended to see different points of view as obstructionism. What with worry and ill health, Captain Luce of the *Glasgow* felt that his friend, no longer his old dynamic self, had no clear concept of what to do.

One Sunday, the padre of *Good Hope* preached ashore, in a service attended by many of the ship's company. After the sermon, the congregation mingled on the cathedral lawn with the officers and men. A young woman noted, "The midshipmen and cadets in their Eton jackets and gold buttons looked such children."

The day before *Canopus* arrived, 21 October, was the 109th anniversary of the RN's most famous victory, the Battle of Trafalgar. The occasion was marked with the usual mess dinner in the wardroom, which the captain and the admiral attended. The midshipmen might have been invited, but if not they celebrated in the same way in the gunroom. After the meal, the health of the king was drunk, seated, followed by the traditional toast of

Old battleship HMS Canopus. *Her heavy armour and 12-inch guns would have leveled the odds, but Cradock remained ignorant of her true speed.*

the day, proposed by the most junior person present, perhaps one of the midshipmen. It being a Wednesday, that toast was "To Ourselves", which was particularly appropriate as they reflected on von Spee's squadron. Proceedings culminated in a toast to "The Immortal Memory" of Admiral Horatio Nelson. Such traditions were at the heart of the RN's will to victory, a psychological advantage which was perhaps its greatest strength. For the moment, difficult as their situation was, those on board scarcely acknowledged the possibility of defeat, even to themselves.

Cradock's flagship Good Hope *(top) and* Monmouth *(bottom). His large cruisers were outclassed by von Spee's* Scharnhorst *and* Gneisenau.

Frustrated, Cradock sailed from the Falklands the day *Canopus* arrived, ordering the battleship to follow the next day, escorting three colliers. *Good Hope* steamed alone through the intricate channels of the Straits of Magellan, the snow-covered mountains and glaciers of Tierra del Fuego shining in the spring sunlight. Through the Straits and in the

Pacific by 26 October, *Good Hope* steered northward toward Valparaiso, 3,460 km (1,250 miles) away.

Meanwhile, von Spee concentrated his five ships at Easter Island: *Scharnhorst, Gneisenau, Dresden, Leipzig* and *Nurnberg*. One of the two European inhabitants, an English rancher unaware a war was on, happily sold the Germans a considerable amount of beef. On 18 October, the squadron sailed, carrying out frequent battle practice while on passage.

They arrived at Más Afuera in the Juan Fernandez Island group on 26 October. Chartered colliers and supply ships awaited them at a small anchorage, under towering 3,000-foot cliffs rising sheer from the water. Von Spee's next port of call would be Valparaiso, less than 750 km (460 miles) to the east. He was informed by the captain of *Dresden* that his ship had been pursued as far as the Magellan Straits by a British squadron consisting of *Good Hope, Monmouth, Glasgow* and *Canopus*. Now able to assess the strength of Cradock's force, the Germans were certain of victory if a battle ensued. According to Pochammer, the officers of *Gneisenau* assembled in the wardroom and drank a toast to the coming engagement.

On the same day, *Good Hope* caught up with *Glasgow, Monmouth* and *Otranto*, and the ships coaled in the secluded inlet of Vallenar in the Chonos Archipelago. Hills several hundred feet high rose steeply from the water's edge. Well covered with evergreen and deciduous trees, they were a welcome sight after the inhospitable barrens of the Falklands and the Straits of Magellan. Silver and Palmer secured leave for a brief and unsuccessful hunting expedition, from which they returned soaking wet after a tumble in a mountain stream. The two squadrons were now within 2000 kilometers of each other, both converging on Valparaiso. Neither knew exactly where the other was, but each had measured the other's strength. A battle was still not inevitable, but the odds against an encounter were rapidly narrowing.

As his ships coaled, Cradock had ample time to consider his course of action. He had learned of a failure by the RN that was to have momentous consequences. In early August 1914, the German battle cruiser *Goeben* was refitting at the Austrian base of Pola in the Adriatic, accompanied by the light cruiser *Breslau,* both apparently neutralized by the superior British and French Mediterranean fleets. As international tension grew, Admiral Souchon eluded British forces and made a successful run for Turkey. *Goeben*'s arrival in Istanbul decided the Turks in favour of Germany against the allies. The supply route to Russia via the Black Sea was cut, a major factor leading to Russian collapse and to the Bolshevik Revolution of 1917.

The last British force with a chance to intercept the fleeing *Goeben* was the First Cruiser Squadron, under the command of Rear-Admiral Ernest Troubridge. His orders prohibited him from engaging

South America, showing critical locations and events.

Admiral Prince Louis of Battenberg, German by birth, professional head of the Royal Navy in 1914. Forced to resign after unfounded charges that he was disloyal.

a superior force. He interpreted that term to include *Goeben* and gave up the pursuit.

At first the admiralty intended to charge him with the shameful offence of cowardice, but changed it to "... failure to pursue an enemy then fleeing." The court martial accepted his superior force argument and honourably acquitted him. Despite his acquittal, Troubridge was not allowed to take up a prestigious appointment promised to him. In fact, he was never employed at sea again. The implication

of cowardice never quite disappeared.

Like Troubridge, Cradock was in command of an independent cruiser squadron, his mission bedeviled by unclear instructions. His colleague's fate sent a pertinent message. Anyone who knew Cradock was certain he would never allow himself to be put in a similar position.

The admiralty itself was in the throes of a major shake up. The First Sea Lord, Prince Louis of Battenberg, was born in a minor German principality. At 14 he acquired British citizenship and joined the RN. His progress was rapid, based on keen intelligence and hard work. The fact that he was married to a granddaughter of Queen Victoria was no hindrance. At the beginning of the war, he was First Sea Lord, the professional head of the navy, and was widely recognized as the best man for the position in the crisis.

It fell to him to manage the inexperienced and overwhelmed admiralty staff, while adapting to the unique management style of his civilian chief, Winston Churchill. Under his direction, the main British Fleet was well positioned to counter the German High Seas Fleet in the North Sea at the beginning of the war. Unfortunately for him, this achievement was overshadowed in the public mind by a series of minor but well-publicized failures, of which the *Goeben* escape was one.

A whispering campaign began, attributing the setbacks to German sympathies on the part of Prince Louis. There had always been some muted resentment of his advancement among a small group of senior naval officers, and now the popular press took up the patriotic cry against him. There is no doubt that he was loyal, and he was strongly supported by Churchill; but he gradually sank into depression under the unwarranted attacks. On 28 October, he resigned and was immediately succeeded by Admiral Sir John Fisher, the eccentric genius who had held the same position from 1904 to 1910.[2]

Thus it was to an admiralty convulsed by change at the top that Cradock addressed his final message on 26 October:

> *With reference to orders to search for enemy and our great desire for early success, consider it impracticable on account of Canopus slow speed to find and destroy enemy squadron. Consequently have ordered Defence to join me after calling at Montevideo for orders. Canopus will be employed in necessary work of convoying colliers.*

By requesting *Defence* and relegating *Canopus* to convoy work, Cradock was recognizing that *Good Hope*, *Monmouth*, and *Glasgow* were no match for von Spee's ships. No doubt he felt that his message made it clear that he nevertheless intended to search for them, without *Canopus*, in hope that he would soon be joined by *Defence*.[3]

Distracted by the resignation of Prince Louis, the admiralty staff did not reach the same conclusion. A combined British and Japanese force, moving south along the west coast of America,

Admiral Sir John "Jacky" Fisher. An eccentric genius, creator of HMS Dreadnought. In 1914 succeeded Prince Louis as First Sea Lord.

prevented von Spee from turning north. Thus, "... he will be forced south on *Glasgow* and *Monmouth* which have good speed and can draw them on to *Good Hope* and *Canopus*, which should keep within supporting distance." The 28 October reply to Cradock's message was: "*Defence* is to remain on east coast under orders of Stoddart. This will leave sufficient force on each side in case hostile cruisers appear on the trade route." Critically, *Canopus* was not mentioned; Cradock's decision to detach it for convoy work seemed to have been accepted, implying that he had "sufficient force" even without the old battleship.

On the evening of 27 October, *Glasgow* left Vallenar to carry mail and pick up signals at the Chilean port of Coronel. Captain Luce successfully argued that Lieutenant Hirst should remain aboard for the Coronel visit rather than joining the admiral. Hirst boarded *Monmouth* and *Good Hope* to pick up their mail. Two officers with whom he had previously served took him aside and gave him farewell messages for their wives saying, "*Glasgow* has got the speed, so she can get away; but we are for it."

The mail leaving the ships contained completed forms signed by all four Canadian midshipmen

Senior officers of the EAS. Von Spee in centre with hand in pocket; on his left his friend Captain Maerker of Gneisenau.

allocating a large fraction of their September pay to their families, instructions that were duly honoured. They must also have written personal letters, taken by *Glasgow* to Coronel to be forwarded with the other squadron mail. Only William Palmer's survived. Apart from complaints about the never-ending coaling, and the absence of mail, it might have been written by a tourist. Out of consideration for his family, there is no hint of the encounter all knew was imminent, nor of the odds against the British.

On 29 October, *Canopus* arrived with the colliers. Captain Grant informed Cradock that he needed 24 hours to repair steam glands. He was told to do so and then follow the squadron.

Grant now learned that his engineer commander laboured under the delusion that the ship's condensers were on the point of total failure. During the voyage south the mentally ill officer never left his cabin, but advised Grant that the ship could not exceed 12 knots. This information was given to Cradock. Eventually, the commander's deputy summoned the courage to tell Grant that the ship could steam at least 15 knots and perhaps faster. Grant did not pass the correction on to Cradock, perhaps thinking that the admiral did not want the old battleship with him anyway, or possibly because by the time he learned the truth, Cradock had imposed radio silence.

Whether Cradock would have waited for *Canopus* or adjusted his plan had he known the fact about its speed is an unanswerable question; after all, he took the 17-knot *Otranto* with him, only two knots faster than *Canopus*' true 15.

On 29 October, *Good Hope*, *Monmouth* and *Otranto* left Vallenar. They were outside wireless range from the Falklands. Cradock still had not received the admiralty message of 28 October, nor would he receive it unless it awaited collection from the British consul in Coronel.

The night before, the East Asiatic Squadron sailed by moonlight from Más Afuera. On 30 October, they saw the glow of the lights of Valparaiso at a distance of about 40 miles. As dawn arose, they sighted the snow-covered peak of Mount Aconcagua, the highest mountain in the Americas. Von Spee detached his colliers and supply vessels to seek temporary shelter in neutral ports, while his light cruisers scattered to intercept allied merchant vessels. Now committed to action, in Commander Pochhammer's words, "officers and crews calmly awaited the events that each man now felt to be imminent."

On the night of 29 October, steaming toward Coronel, *Glasgow* heard wireless transmissions from *Leipzig*, the tone of the German Telefunken signal being different from that of the Marconi system in British service. The technology did not exist to determine the bearing of the transmitting ship, but experienced operators could estimate her distance by the strength of the signal. *Leipzig* was believed to be within 150 miles of *Glasgow*, information which was passed to Cradock

At 6:30 p.m., 31 October, *Glasgow* anchored in the harbour of Coronel and the British consul boarded, bringing news of the fighting on land and sea and stressing the capabilities of the German intelligence organization in Chile. In fact, as soon as *Glasgow* anchored, a German merchant ship in the harbour sent a boat ashore and shortly afterwards a beacon burst into flames on a nearby hill. Meanwhile, the news was telegraphed to the German consul at Valparaiso. At 3:00 a.m. on 1 November, von Spee received a wireless message that *Glasgow* was at Coronel. He collected his squadron

SMS Leipzig. *Von Spee ordered all his ships to use* Leipzig's *call sign, causing Cradock to believe it was the only German ship near Coronel.*

Churchill and Fisher on the steps of the Admiralty. They worked well in tandem until the Dardanelles disaster of 1915.

ship within wireless range. Meanwhile, Cradock ordered radio silence for his squadron, so the only firm intelligence von Spee had was the eyewitness report that *Glasgow* was at Coronel. Each admiral was under the impression that he was likely to encounter only one enemy light cruiser and not his entire force.

Over the night of 31 October, the wind increased to near gale force from the south, raising high seas in the offshore waters. Plunging their bows directly into the rising billows, von Spee's ships were forced to reduce speed to allow the smaller cruisers to keep up. In Coronel harbour, Captain Luce was aware that his location was revealed and that he risked being trapped. It took time to dispatch the mail and telegrams and decode the signals brought by the consul, and it was not until 9:15 a.m. on Sunday, 1 November, that *Glasgow* sailed. To deceive unfriendly watchers Luce first steered north-west, altering when out of sight of land to the south-west, toward a pre-arranged rendezvous with the rest of the squadron.

At the rendezvous, the sea was so rough that it was impossible to lower boats to transfer the mails and messages picked up at Coronel. The most important were sealed in a cask that *Glasgow* towed across the bow of *Good Hope*, to be grappled and hauled aboard.[4] Always the professional seaman, Cradock congratulated both ships with the flag signal, "Manoeuver well executed."

Assuming that *Leipzig* was operating alone and was not far away, at about 2:00 p.m. Cradock ordered his squadron into a search line, with 15 miles between ships, speed 10 knots, course northwest by north. *Glasgow* was the easternmost ship, with *Otranto* next, then *Monmouth*, and, finally, *Good Hope* at the western end.

Then Cradock retired to his cabin to read his

and increased speed to 14 knots, steering to the south, well offshore, to intercept the British ship as it left the port.

Ironically, both admirals underestimated the strength of their enemy. Von Spee had directed all his ships to use the *Leipzig's* call sign, deceiving the British, who thought it was the only German

SMS Gneisenau, *armoured cruiser*

messages. For the first time, he saw the admiralty signal of 28 October: "*Defence* is to remain on east, coast …. This will leave sufficient force on each side in case hostile cruisers appear on the trade route." He believed that the admiralty understood that he had detached *Canopus.* Therefore, this message meant that, even without the battleship, he was deemed to have sufficient force to deal with von Spee.

Churchill and Fisher had discussed the overall naval situation in the Admiralty War Room, with a gigantic world map covering one wall. Churchill betrayed some uncertainty about Cradock's intentions. As he recounts in *The World Crisis*, he queried the admiral, "You don't suppose he would

try to fight them without the *Canopus*?" To this, Churchill says, "He [Fisher] did not give any decided reply." Knowing Cradock better than Churchill, Fisher must have suspected that his answer was an unqualified "Yes."

Despite the near gale, the sun shone brightly on the tumbling seas. In the German squadron, church services were held. Von Spee detached his light cruisers to stop and examine merchant shipping. About 4:00 p.m., wireless transmissions from several British ships were detected. Von Spee recalled his scattered cruisers and dispatched *Dresden* to search ahead.

Routinely, the Germans closed up their gunnery teams every day at 4:00 p.m. to check communications and equipment before nightfall. Just as they were about to stand down the alarm was given, and at 4:20 action stations were assumed.

About 4:00 p.m., *Glasgow*, even before reaching its search station, observed smoke to the north and altered course to investigate. Not long afterwards three ships were sighted, identified as two four-funnelled cruisers and one three-funnelled cruiser: *Scharnhorst, Gneisenau* and *Dresden*, which Luce had believed was the *Leipzig*, whose supposed transmissions had lured the British into a trap. Turning away at full speed, Luce attempted to inform Cradock, but the Germans succeeded in jamming his wireless signals until about 4:25, when his signal, "enemy cruisers in sight steering SSE," reached the bridge of the flagship.[5]

Even with the enemy in sight, Cradock could still have decided not to fight. Darkness was only three hours away. In the days before radar, locating a darkened force at night was largely a matter of chance. Moreover, a surprise close-range encounter would have negated von Spee's gunnery superiority. When contact was made, the three leading

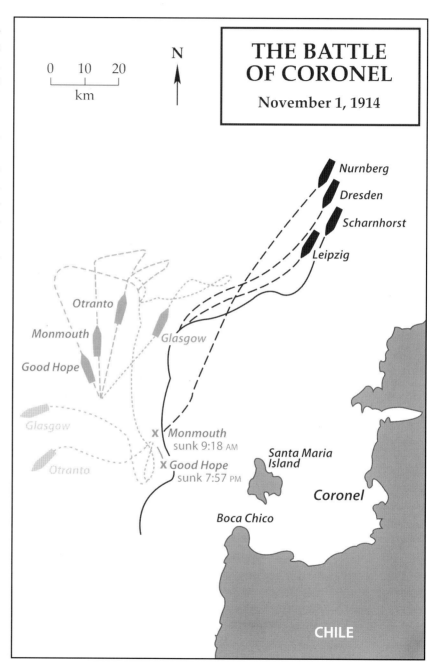

THE BATTLE OF CORONEL

November 1, 1914

Nurnberg
Dresden
Scharnhorst
Leipzig

Otranto

Monmouth

Glasgow

Good Hope

Glasgow

X Monmouth
sunk 9:18 AM

Otranto

X Good Hope
sunk 7:57 PM

Santa Maria
Island

Coronel

Boca Chico

CHILE

The Battle of Coronel

German ships were 12 nautical miles or 24,000 yards away. *Leipzig* and *Nurnberg* were well astern of them. *Glasgow* was the fastest ship in either squadron, and *Good Hope* and *Monmouth* had a small speed advantage over the two enemy armoured cruisers. Although Cradock did not know it, von Spee's ships had taken some of their boilers off-line to save coal. It would take time for them to work up to full speed.

Cradock's decision to take *Otranto* with him as he searched north reduced the maximum speed of his force from 23 to 17 knots. At von Spee's best speed, 22 knots, he could overtake the British at a rate of five nautical miles (10,000 yards) per hour. Thus, after one hour he would have closed to 14,000 yards, just 500 yards outside the extreme range of the 12 8.2-inch guns of his armoured cruisers, with two hours of daylight still ahead of him to destroy the British squadron.

Leaving *Otranto* would have allowed Cradock's remaining ships to draw von Spee toward the *Canopus*, 250 miles to the south, lumbering north at the 15 knots Cradock never learned about. It is doubtful the admiral even considered that course of action. It would have been unthinkable to leave *Otranto* to fend for herself, even though scuttling or an honourable surrender to overwhelming force were options available to the captain.

In a tale full of "might have beens," Cradock's handling of *Otranto* was perhaps the most baffling mystery of all. Its sole value lay in extending his daytime search line by an additional 15 miles. Once the enemy was located, the ship became a liability, too weakly armed to play any role in an

Von Spee's flagship SMS Scharnhorst *easily out-duelled* Good Hope.

engagement, too slow to either retreat from or pursue the enemy. There is little doubt that Cradock had concluded that, whenever he met von Spee, he was bound to be defeated, regardless of which motley group of ships he had with him. But von Spee was far from any base where he could refit. Even while going down to defeat, if he could inflict damage on the German ships, Cradock might neutralize their threat until reinforcements arrived. Most likely, this scenario had become his aim, rather than the victory he knew he could never win. If so, finding the German squadron was paramount and in this *Otranto* could be helpful. Once found, the result was in the hands of fate.

Cradock ordered his ships to form line of battle on a southerly course, in the order *Good Hope, Monmouth, Glasgow* and *Otranto. Glasgow* and *Otranto* were closing the flagship and now

Armed Merchant Cruiser Otranto. *Slow and weakly armed, its presence severely limited Cradock's tactical options.*

Monmouth steered to take position in the line. In response to the action alarm the men hastened to their stations. An observer in *Otranto* later told William Palmer's family "The crew of the *Good Hope* were great lads alright, as they steamed past us to take the lead they cheered and cheered, and we cheered them."

The duties assigned to the four midshipmen in *Good Hope* can be guessed with some confidence. One of them probably reported to the bridge as action midshipman of the watch. In *Berwick*, all had qualified to take charge of a 6-inch gun and now one or two mustered their gun's crews and prepared their weapon for action. At least one was part of the ship's fire control team, assisting the gunnery officer in the director platform high up the mainmast, or locked in the transmitting station below the armoured deck.

In *Gneisenau*, Pochammer did a final check of the ship, noting that the guns were pointing toward the enemy, cocked up to maximum elevation, even though still well out of range. His own station was in the control room, a steel-armoured compartment three decks directly below the bridge, connected to it by an armoured trunking. As the ship's executive officer, he coordinated damage control, firefighting, and casualty treatment should the ship be hit. At the same time, he followed the tactical situation, since all wheel and engine room orders passed through the control room, and gunnery fire control communications were monitored there. If his captain was killed or wounded, he would climb through the trunking and take charge on the bridge.

A tactical duel ensued between the two admirals. Before battle commenced each tried to obtain a position technically known as gunnery advantage, having regard to weather, visibility, sea state and other factors. Both realized that the critical factor was the relative positions of the two squadrons at the time of sunset. As the sun neared the horizon, the force furthest to the west had the advantage because the sun's rays shone directly into the eyes of the enemy gun aimers. However, as soon as it dipped below the horizon the advantage dramatically reversed for a short period because the westernmost force, silhouetted against the afterglow, was a perfect target. while the eastern gradually faded into the gathering gloom.

The sun would set at 6:50 p.m. At 6:00 p.m. the Germans were on Cradock's port quarter, both squadrons heading south. Cradock's initial plan was to alter course to port to lead his squadron across the enemy bows, a maneuver known as "crossing the T," that allowed all his guns to fire on the leading ship, which could only reply with its forward turret. He ordered his ships to turn 45 degrees to port. Thanks to his superior speed, von Spee easily thwarted this manoeuver by also altering course to port, keeping Cradock on his beam. Cradock returned to his southerly course. By this time *Leipzig* rejoined von Spee and *Nurnberg* was quickly catching up.

With his enemy looking into the sun, now about 8 degrees above the horizon, Cradock achieved a temporary position of gunnery advantage and seized his only chance. At 6:18 he signalled to *Canopus*, "I am going to attack the enemy now," increased his squadron's speed to *Otranto's* maximum 17 knots, and steered inward to close the range. Again, von Spee foiled him by altering away, and Cradock returned to his southerly course, well aware of what would follow.

With a five knot speed advantage, von Spee dictated the time of engagement. At 6:50, just as the sun set, he turned ten degrees toward the British

Scharnhorst's *forward turret, showing twin 8.2" guns*

line, the outlines of Cradock's ships etched sharply against the still-bright western horizon. In his control room, Pochammer heard the range takers in *Scharnhorst's* director tower counting down every 100 metres, in the calm tones they had been trained to use in their many drills: "Hundred fifteen hectometers, hundred fourteen hectometers, hundred twelve hectometres." At 7:04 both Germans armoured cruisers opened fire with salvos from their 8.2-inch guns, *Scharnhorst* on *Good Hope* and *Gneisenau* on *Monmouth*, at a range of 11,400 yards. Commander Pochammer had time to reflect that not long ago *Monmouth* had been *Gneisenau's* host ship in Hong Kong: "We had fraternized with her officers … and in all friendliness drunk the health of our respective sovereigns at meals. Joyous times! Now we were again to shout hurrahs, but only when she should disappear beneath the waves."

Artist's conception of Good Hope *shortly before blowing up and disappearing with all hands.*

Good Hope replied with a single sighting shot from one of its 9.2-inch turrets. The 6-inch guns in all ships were still out of range. Cradock belatedly ordered *Otranto* to leave the line of battle, where it contributed nothing.

From *Glasgow*'s bridge, Lieutenant Hirst had a perfect view of the enemy line and of the two British cruisers ahead.[6] He observed a textbook example of gunnery efficiency. *Scharnhorst*'s first salvo

was deliberately aimed to land 500 metres short of *Good Hope*. Its splash confirmed that it was directly in line with the target. The sights were raised by 1,000 metres for the second salvo, which hit in line with *Good Hope*, but 500 metres over. The range was reduced by 500 metres and the third salvo achieved a direct hit on the forward 9.2-inch turret, which was left a furiously blazing twisted mess. Half of *Good Hope*'s main armament was already out of action. *Gneisenau*'s first salvo straddled *Monmouth*, and the second scored a direct hit.

Good Hope was firing one round a minute from the after 9.2-inch turret. None of the British 6-inch guns were yet within range, but it was obvious that those on the main decks of the two armoured cruisers could not be used in the steep head seas, which were breaking over the ships' bridges and causing even the heavy cruisers to roll and pitch as though possessed. The Germans faced the same problem, but to a lesser extent, since their casemated guns were at least one deck higher. At 7:05, *Glasgow* opened fire on *Leipzig* with two 6-inch guns, but was unable to spot the fall of shot in the gathering darkness. By now the enemy ships were no more than vague shapes against the evening gloom. The Germans scored hit after hit on *Good Hope* and *Monmouth*, silhouetted like targets in a shooting gallery. Each time a shell struck their upper works their sides shimmered with an orange glow and blazing flames were seen through holes smashed in their sides.

In a desperate attempt to bring the 6-inch batteries into action, Cradock managed to close the range to 5,000 yards, but the German 6-inch guns were now in action, too. The German ships fired four salvos a minute against clearly visible targets, while the British aimed only at the enemy gun flashes. At 7:14, with the fore turret on fire, *Monmouth* staggered to starboard of the British line, but remained in action. Lieutenant Hirst remembered:

Good Hope and Monmouth were now on either bow of Glasgow, and the smoke from their funnels was reddened by the dull glare of the deck-fires below. On their far side the "overs" showed high white splashes against the darkening sky, and the columns of water thrown up by the "shorts" were yellowed by the discharges from our guns. Frequently either ship flashed into a vivid orange as a lyddite shell detonated against her upper works.

Ears had become deadened by the roar of our guns and almost insensible to the shriek of fragments flying overhead from the shells which burst short. The enemy's ships were no longer visible, and the gun layers, when the motion of the ship allowed them, could aim only through the zone of splashes between the lines at the flashes of the enemy guns.

Obviously in trouble, *Monmouth* hauled out further to starboard, while *Good Hope* steered directly toward the enemy, perhaps in a desperate attempt to ram or launch torpedoes. Apparently, someone on the flagship's bridge was still thinking, orders were still being given and obeyed, and, despite terrible punishment, the ship was still steaming and answering the rudder. But at 7:50, an 8.2-inch shell struck between the mainmast and the

German medallion commemorating von Spee's victory, showing him and his sons Otto and Heinrich.

after funnel, followed almost immediately by a terrific explosion, which flung flame and debris more than 200 feet in the air. One of the after 6-inch casemates fired twice more, then *Good Hope* fell silent, "… gutted of her upper works, and only lighted by a dull red glow which shortly disappeared."

Scharnhorst joined *Gneisenau* in firing at *Monmouth*, while *Glasgow* shifted from *Leipzig* to *Gneisenau* and obtained one 6-inch hit. When *Monmouth* ceased fire both enemy armoured cruisers concentrated on *Glasgow*, but by now it was so dark that they failed to hit. *Monmouth* slowly turned away, badly down by the bows.

Night had fallen and none of the British ships were visible. Von Spee ordered his squadron to cease fire and his light cruisers to search for the enemy.

Alone, *Glasgow* circled to the north in search of *Monmouth*, finding it low in the water, but with fires apparently under control. By flashing light, Luce asked, "Are you all right?" and received the reply, "I want to get stern to sea. I am taking water badly forward." Detecting suspicious shapes in the darkness, Luce asked, "Can you steer NW? The enemy are following us astern." Receiving no reply, Luce had to make an agonizing decision. The thought of abandoning a ship to certain destruction was devastating, but in the high seas *Glasgow* could not render effective assistance. If overtaken, *Glasgow* would be destroyed, and it was essential to warn *Canopus*. Reluctantly, Luce gave the order to withdraw to the northwest at full speed. As *Glasgow* departed, the men on the deck of *Monmouth* cheered. Despite being under fire for more than an hour, *Glasgow* received only five hits, four of which exploded uselessly in coal bunkers. Only four men were slightly wounded.

One final act remained. By the time the main action ended, *Nurnberg* had not yet caught up to the German squadron and had little knowledge of the tactical situation. Stumbling upon the crippled *Monmouth*, its fore turret missing, lying low in the water, but still flying the ensign and slowly making way, *Nurnberg* shone a searchlight on the ensign and fired several warning shots over the ship to give the crew an opportunity to surrender. When there was no reaction a torpedo was launched, which missed. At this point officers in *Monmouth* were heard recalling their men to their guns. The Germans had no choice but to manoeuver under the stern and sink the battered ship with point-blank fire from the 4.1-inch guns. The fleeing *Glasgow* heard 75 shots, then silence. The *Monmouth* and 675 men went down at 8:58 with flag still flying. The seas were too high to lower boats, and unidentified ships (actually German) were approaching. *Nurnberg* drew away without attempting to rescue survivors, an act for which the captain was criticized by the British until the full story was known.

In little over an hour, von Spee's ships convincingly defeated a British squadron, the first such defeat in more than 100 years, a remarkable achievement for a navy that was scarcely 20 years old. Von Spee signaled: "With God's help a glorious victory, for which I express my recognition and congratulations to the crews."

Good Hope was ablaze, and ceased firing after the mammoth explosion, but no one in the German ships actually saw the ship go down. *Leipzig* steered for a dull glow, but reaching the spot nothing was seen from the bridge. Later, the captain learned that men on deck had seen debris in the waves; but by the time he was told any chance of rescue had long passed.

Von Spee did not immediately realize the magnitude of his success. Conceivably, *Good Hope* remained afloat and escaped in the darkness or, perhaps, beached on the coast. Joined by Chilean vessels, the Germans searched for two days, but not a trace was ever found of the flagship, the admiral, 900 men, or the Royal Canadian Navy's first dead.

Chapter 5
FULL CIRCLE

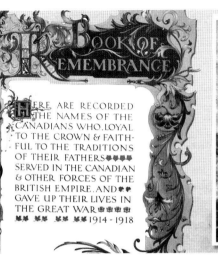

On 3 November the Admiralty received information from the consul-general at Valparaiso that at the end of October at least three German cruisers were operating in the vicinity. Churchill wrote: "Here at last was the vital message for which the Admiralty Staff had waited so long. Admiral von Spee's squadron was definitely located on the West Coast of South America. He had not slipped past Admiral Cradock round the Horn as had been possible." The British force on the east coast could now be drawn upon to reinforce Cradock. Admiral Stoddart was ordered to detach *Defence* to proceed with all possible dispatch to join him.

On the evening of 3 November, a message was sent to Cradock informing him of this plan and instructing:

Glasgow should find or keep in touch with the enemy. You should keep touch with Glasgow concentrating the rest of your squadron including Canopus. It is important you should effect your junction with Defence at earliest possible moment subject to keeping touch with Glasgow and enemy.

But, in Churchill's words, "... we were already talking to the void." At 7:00 a.m., 4 November, he opened a dispatch from the consul-general at Valparaiso:

Have just learned from Chilean admiral that German admiral states that on Sunday at sunset, in thick and wicked weather, his ships met Good Hope, Glasgow, Monmouth and Otranto.

Action was joined, and Monmouth turned over and sank after an hour's fighting. Good Hope, Glasgow and Otranto drew off into darkness. Good Hope was on fire, an explosion was heard, and she is believed to have sunk.

Then and later, Churchill and the admiralty declined to accept any responsibility for Cradock's defeat. In their opinion, the fault was entirely his for mishandling his squadron, accepting battle without the assistance of the invulnerable *Canopus*, and allowing his force to be handicapped by the useless *Otranto*. However, when questioned in Parliament, Churchill attempted to attach a logical rationale to the admiral's actions:

… we are of the opinion that feeling that he could not bring the enemy immediately to action as long as he kept with the Canopus, he decided to attack them with his fast ships alone, in the belief that even if he himself were destroyed in the action, he would inflict damage upon them which in the circumstances would be irreparable, and lead to their certain destruction.

In fact, the two German armoured cruisers suffered few hits, none of which impaired them in the slightest. The light cruisers were unscathed, and only two men were slightly wounded in *Gneisenau*. Of more importance, the two armoured cruisers

Scharnhorst, Gneisenau *and* Nurnberg *in Valparaiso after their victory. Chilean warships in foreground.*

Armoured cruisers Scharnhorst *and* Gneisenau *in Valparaiso.*

expended more than 40 percent of their 8.2-inch ammunition, which could not be replenished short of Germany.

The fact remained that the RN's prestige suffered a severe blow and there now seemed no barrier to von Spee emerging on the South Atlantic trade routes. The disaster captured international interest. On 5 November, the *New York Times* commented that the defeat was the sensation of the hour: "That the Germans were able to sink or scatter the British squadron, with only minor damage to their own ships and a casualty list of only two wounded, is a source of wonder." Vice-Admiral Sir David Beatty, one of Britain's most notable naval commanders, observed. "Poor old Kit Cradock has gone at Coronel. His death and the loss of the ships and the gallant lives in them can be laid to the door of the incompetency of the Admiralty. They have broken over and over again the first principles of strategy." Coming on top of previous naval reverses, the disaster caused a political storm in Britain.

As will be seen, under the impetus of the new First Sea Lord the admiralty's reaction was swift.

News of the battle spread slowly. In the early months of the war, Canadian newspapers were full of the campaign in France. The few minor naval actions were covered, but everyone waited for the decisive battle in the North Sea, in which the RN would of course win the war for the allies.[1]

On 5 November, the Halifax *Herald* reported rumours of a battle off the coast of Chile, but the admiralty could not confirm that one had taken place. The next issue acknowledged that a battle had occurred, but stated that *Good Hope* had not taken part. Not until 7 November did the paper print the true story, under the headline: "WE WILL NEVER FORGET OUR FOUR BRAVE BOYS." The inside pages carried pictures of the Halifax natives William Palmer and Arthur Silver, and also of *Good Hope* and *Monmouth*. The paper noted, "As H.M.S. *Good Hope* was at Halifax early in the war her loss causes particular sorrow here.

ROLL OF HONOR. CANADIAN NAVAL SERVICE – Passed with H.M.S. Good Hope in Southern Seas, while fighting for the Empire. No. 1 Midshipman Silver, Halifax, N.S.; No. 2 Midshipman Palmer, Halifax, N.S.; No. 3 Midshipman Cann, Yarmouth, N.S.; No. 4 Midshipman Hatheway, Fredericton, N.B.

"Roll of Honour." Front page of the Montreal Star, 5 November 1914.

When this cruiser steamed up Halifax harbour on August 14 her crew lined the deck and with the ship's band playing patriotic airs she was the object of interest to those on the waterfront."

The headline in the Montreal *Star* on 4 November, proclaimed: "GOOD HOPE REPORTED SAFE AFTER NAVAL FIGHT WHERE GERMANS CLAIM THEY SUNK MONMOUTH." A reference to von Spee's squadron appeared in the Fredericton *Gleaner* on 2 November, captioned, "Germans Coal From Chile by Stealth." The article carried no hint of a battle, one day

after Coronel had actually been fought. On the 4th, the paper headlined: "THE GOOD HOPE MAY HAVE BEEN BLOWN ON ROCKS OF SOUTH AMERICAN COAST BY HURRICANE." In smaller type below, "British fought heroically but were out of class. Pounded at long range. Were seriously damaged before Guns reached the Foe." Apart from the uncertainty about *Good Hope*, the *Gleaner* had a good idea how the battle had gone. In a sidebar it named the four midshipmen and their home towns.

On 7 November the Yarmouth *Light* published a War Extra, announcing, "GOOD HOPE LOST, AND MONMOUTH BADLY DAMAGED IN SUNDAY'S BATTLE ACCORDING TO LATEST ADMIRALTY REPORTS." The paper printed the names and addresses of the four lost midshipmen and observed, "There will be profound sympathy for the parents of those boys, but they have the consolation of knowing they gave themselves for their country, and their names have been inscribed in the honor role of our glorious Empire." One hundred Yarmouth men had already volunteered for the army, and in the weeks immediately following Malcolm Cann's death another 100 did so.

A week later the midshipmen's families received a message of sympathy from King George V and Queen Mary: "The King and Queen deeply regret the loss you and the navy have sustained by the death of your son in the service of his country. Their majesties truly sympathize with you in your sorrow." The *Herald* commented:

> … *none of these four midshipmen was over twenty years of age, and their death, though it was in the service of Empire, is particularly pathetic. They are among the first of Canada's youth to be numbered in the present war as*

ones who have died for their country. These four midshipmen are indeed the first of those in the Canadian Naval Service to give their lives for the Empire.

Actually, they were the first in any Canadian service to die in what became known as the Great War. As the struggle went on, casualties in the trench warfare in France became so heavy that individual deaths no longer figured in press reports.

Interestingly, the royal message makes no reference to Empire, referring only to service to country. Perhaps their majesties foresaw the loosening of the bonds that gathered momentum during and after, and largely because of, the war.

Families were not officially informed of their loss until 13 November, in a telegram signed by the Chief of the Naval Service, Rear-Admiral Kingsmill: "I regret to inform you HMS *Good Hope* was lost with all hands after an action with a German Squadron off the coast of Chile, on Sunday the 1st November." This terse announcement was followed by a slightly more heartfelt letter from J.D. Hazen, Minister for the Naval Service:[2]

I am writing to express my deepest sympathy with you in the loss of your son recently in H.M.S. GOOD HOPE. I understand that he was chosen for that Ship especially by the Rear-Admiral Commanding, on account of the general excellence of his work, and that fact, together with the noble manner of his death, must be a source of gratification to you and will, I am sure, tend to help you to bear your loss. I trust you will accept the sympathy of me and the Department of the Naval Service generally, in your grief.

TOP: Von Spee's boat arriving alongside Valparaiso landing stage. BOTTOM: Von Spee met by von Eckerdt, German ambassador to Chile.

Despite these official notices, the mothers of Malcolm Cann and Arthur Silver never accepted that their sons had died.

Meanwhile, the proud German squadron enjoyed the fruits of its victory. After his unsuccessful

Admiral von Spee's triumphal progress through the streets of Valparaiso.

two-day search for traces of the *Good Hope*, von Spee led his ships into Valparaiso on 3 November. Shore leave was granted to the officers in relays and fresh provisions were embarked in the 24 hours that the squadron was permitted to stay under international law. German visitors were allowed on board and merchant seamen from German vessels in the harbour volunteered to join the squadron.

The admiral was met by the German Ambassador and received a hero's welcome from the largely pro-German civilian population that included numerous German immigrants. Von Spee's own mood was far from triumphant. At a reception given in his honour by the German community, the toast was proposed: "Damnation to the British Navy." Von Spee rose and in the silence said sternly: "I drink to a brave and honourable foe," took his hat and left the function, followed by his officers. At the door, a woman offered him a bouquet of flowers, which he accepted, saying, "They will

do for my grave." A retired naval doctor and old friend now living in Valparaiso saw von Spee, who confided prophetically, "I must plough the seas of the world doing as much harm as I can, till my ammunition is exhausted, or till a foe far superior in power succeeds in catching me."

Despite the victory, von Spee's basic situation had not changed. He had defeated one British squadron, but he could well imagine new forces concentrating against him, and he was far from home. He returned to Más Afuera, where his ships coaled from captured colliers for 36 hours at a stretch, in suffocating heat. There seemed no need to hurry. After a leisurely passage, on 19 November the squadron coaled in the Gulf of Penas, 875 miles south of Valparaiso. By that day von Spee had settled on his course of action and signalled Berlin: "The German squadron intends to break through to home."

The morning after the battle, *Glasgow* rendezvoused with *Canopus* and the two ships steamed at full speed for the Falklands. *Otranto* managed to escape to Montevideo. On 9 November, *Canopus* and *Glasgow* sailed for the River Plate on admiralty orders, but two days later the battleship was ordered back to organize the defence of Port Stanley. During *Canopus'* absence, the Germans obtained intelligence that the Falklands were undefended, information that reached von Spee.

Although he had no illusions about the difficulties ahead, von Spee would have been astonished had he known of the forces to be unleashed against him. At 1:00 p.m. London time, on 4 November,

Admiral Jellicoe, in command of the Grand Fleet, was ordered to detach the battle cruisers *Invincible* and *Inflexible* to coal and proceed to Plymouth "for foreign service." The British and German fleets in home waters were very evenly balanced, but Churchill and Fisher decided to risk doing without these powerful vessels temporarily. With eight 12-inch guns each and speeds of 25.5 knots, the battle cruisers could both far outrun and outfight von Spee's armoured cruisers.

Vice-Admiral Sir Doveton Sturdee was Chief of Staff at the admiralty, with responsibility for "Distribution of the Fleet in sufficient strength to meet the enemy." He participated in the questionable decision-making that culminated at Coronel. He and Fisher had long been at odds and the new First Sea Lord refused to work with him. The problem was neatly solved by placing Sturdee in command in the South Atlantic, with the mission of avenging Coronel. The battle cruisers were inspected at Plymouth on 9 November and in view of numerous defects the dockyard declared that they could not be made ready to proceed until 13 November. This occasioned a tough message from Churchill to the admiral superintendent, and Sturdee left Plymouth as ordered on 11 November.

Unaware of the gathering storm, von Spee moved southward and eastward at a deliberate pace, taking every opportunity to coal. Morale was given a boost when the Kaiser awarded the Iron Cross 1st Class to von Spee, and the Iron Cross 2nd Class to 300 personnel. Among the number was one of von Spee's sons. In general, however, the mood was fatalistic, akin to the feeling in Cradock's ships as they passed through the same waters in the opposite direction a few short weeks before.

Approaching the Straits of Magellan, the squadron ran into a terrible storm. Waves reached 30

TOP: *Vice-Admiral Sir Frederick Doveton Sturdee, commander of the RN squadron despatched to avenge Coronel.* BOTTOM: *Forward 12-inch guns of HMS Inflexible, with 6-inch gun atop B turret.*

HMS Invincible, *Sturdee's flagship. Note tripod masts characteristic of British dreadnoughts.*

metres and much of the extra coal stored on the upper decks was lost overboard. When the squadron captured the Canadian collier *Drummuir*, with 2,500 tons aboard, the opportunity was taken to fully replenish at an anchorage in the Beagle Channel.

Sturdee arrived at the Abrolhos Rocks coaling harbour, where he rendezvoused with Stoddart's cruisers, including *Glasgow*. His mission was cloaked in secrecy, but because of coaling at the Cape Verde Islands, his presence in the South Atlantic became known. Lieutenant Hirst heard it discussed openly by British civilians at the Club Centrale in Rio de Janeiro, while a party of Germans dined at the next table. For once, German intelligence proved inefficient. The news never reached von Spee. On the other hand, Sturdee learned that von Spee was in the Straits of Magellan.

Sturdee left Albrohos on 28 November. His squadron consisted of the battle cruisers *Invincible* (flagship) and *Inflexible*, the armoured cruisers *Carnarvon*, *Kent*, and *Cornwall*, and the light cruiser *Glasgow*. His destination was the Falkland Islands, where he would coal in preparation for a major search for von Spee. To conceal the presence of the battle cruisers, he transmitted his wireless traffic from *Carnarvon*.

Brilliant at Coronel, von Spee's tactical instincts had dulled by the time his squadron reached the Atlantic. Before starting the next leg of his homeward journey, he had to replenish his bunkers. A misleading message from Montevideo led him to believe that little if any coal was available at the rendezvous arranged off Puerto Santa Elena on the coast of Patagonia. Believing that Port Stanley

Eye-witness watercolour of Canopus' *shells landing short of* Gneisenau *and* Nurnberg. *Smoke from remaining German vessels in distance.*

was undefended, he determined to attack. If he occupied the port, even briefly, his coal problem was solved and the island might be garrisoned by German volunteers from Argentina, forcing the British to make a major effort to recover it. At worst he could destroy the coal stores and wireless station, another huge blow to British prestige. Against the advice of most of his senior officers, including his friend Captain Maerker of *Gneisenau*, von Spee determined to make the attempt. On the afternoon of 6 December, the East Asiatic Squadron left the Beagle Channel for the Falklands.

Captain Grant of *Canopus* had done everything possible to strengthen Port Stanley's defences. His old battleship was moved to the inner harbour and deliberately grounded behind hills with the upper masts struck down, making it invisible from seaward. The gunnery fire control system was connected by telephone with a director position on a distant height of land, Elaborate arrangements were made for passing ranges and bearings to the ship and providing spotting corrections for the 12-inch guns. Some of the smaller guns were landed and emplaced ashore. The local militia was strengthened by marines and blue jackets and a makeshift mine barrier was improvised across the harbour entrance.

The people of the Falkland Islands and the crew of *Canopus* felt very much alone as they awaited events in the days after Coronel. Preparing to defend the colony they found time to remember their fallen countrymen. As the Falkland *Magazine and Church Paper* reported:

> *On Sunday November 29th a memorial service was held in the Cathedral, attended by HE the Governor and his Council, the captain, officers, and 150 men from the Canopus, and the officers and men of the Falkland Island Volunteers. Every seat was occupied. It was decided to devote the offerings of this service towards erection of a Memorial Tablet in the Cathedral in order to commemorate those who lost their lives fighting for King and Empire in the naval battle of Coronel. The amount collected is just over £17. Three buglers from the Canopus ended the Service by sounding the "Last Post" in the Nave of the Cathedral.*

Kent, Glasgow *and* Invincible *getting underway in pursuit, as seen from* Inflexible.

Although no secret in Rio de Janeiro, Sturdee's presence in the South Atlantic was not communicated to Grant. When the squadron appeared over the horizon on the afternoon of 7 December, his surprise was total, mingled with relief. One by one the great ships entered the outer harbour and anchored. Notice for steam was increased, and *Carnarvon* was given permission to draw all her fires to effect boiler repairs. The squadron commenced coaling in rotation at 5:30 a.m. on the 8th.

The German squadron approached, as ignorant of Sturdee's arrival as Grant had been. While the remainder lay off to the south, von Spee detached *Gneisenau* and *Nurnberg* to bombard the wireless station at dawn and then enter the harbour. Under the cover of *Nurnberg*'s guns a landing party from *Gneisenau* would destroy the coal depot and try to capture the governor.[3]

Winds were light and visibility was excellent as dawn revealed the low hills surrounding Port Stanley. On board *Gneisenau*, the landing party mustered on deck in white gaiters and carrying rifles. At 7:35 the two ships were spotted by a civilian lookout on Sapper Hill, who telephoned *Canopus*: "a four funnel and a two funnel man of war steering northwards." It was some time later that *Gneisenau* and *Nurnberg* were identified and word passed to Admiral Sturdee, who was shaving in his cabin. He ordered the squadron to raise steam for full speed and then went to breakfast.

Von Spee had achieved complete surprise. Had his full squadron been on the spot, he might have inflicted severe damage even to the battle cruisers before Sturdee's ships had steam enough to manoeuver, or waited at the harbour entrance to engage the British as they emerged one by one.

From the bridge of *Gneisenau*, smoke was observed rising from the funnels of several ships, which was reported to von Spee, but at first no particular alarm was aroused. When the ship's gunnery officer climbed to the spotting top, he discerned two sets of tripod masts, a distinguishing feature of dreadnoughts. His report to Maerker was disregarded because there could be no such ships in the South Atlantic. Von Spee was not informed.

The two German ships reached the position from which they intended to bombard the wireless station. Suddenly, two enormous water spouts arose 1,000 yards away. Directed from the shore, the invisible *Canopus* fired the forward 12-inch guns at their maximum range. A second salvo fell short, but a ricochet pierced *Gneisenau*'s forward funnel. Maerker pressed on to engage the cruiser *Kent*, which was coming out of harbour. For a few minutes, visions of another Coronel

"Der Lezte Mann" ("The Last Man"), German postcard, not historically accurate but representative of the spirit on both sides.

flashed through the minds of the German officers. But, when von Spee was informed of the warships, he immediately ordered the advanced ships to withdraw at full speed and rejoin the squadron. Though still unaware of the British battle cruisers, there was nothing to be gained by another fight with armoured cruisers, now apparently accompanied by at least one old battleship.

Following *Kent*, *Glasgow* was the first of Sturdee's ships to pursue the fleeing Germans. Shortly after 10:00 a.m., the speedier *Invincible* and *Inflexible* overtook with battle ensigns hoisted, black smoke pouring from the funnels, and enormous bow waves

spreading from the stems. Hirst wrote: "No more glorious moment in the war do I remember than when the flagship hoisted the signal 'General Chase.' Fifteen miles to the eastward lay the same ships we had fought at Coronel and which had sent brave Admiral Cradock and our comrades to their deaths."

All telescopes on the *Gneisenau*'s bridge were fixed on the pursuers. Soon it could not be denied that the two leading ships had tripod masts. As Pochammer wrote, they faced "... the possibility, even probability, that we were being chased by English battle cruisers ... this was a very bitter pill for us to swallow. We choked a little ... the throat contracted

Artist's conception of the last moments of Gneisenau.

and stiffened, for it meant a life and death struggle, or rather a fight ending in honourable death."

The Germans were about 12 miles ahead of Sturdee, who enjoyed at least a five knot speed advantage. For once, the weather was perfect and the extreme visibility amazed those present. The British admiral took his time and used his speed and the longer range of his guns to engage the enemy under advantageous conditions, just as von Spee had done at Coronel. Around 11:30, he slackened speed and sent his crews to lunch, many of them still in their filthy coaling rig. Most consumed their sandwiches on the weather decks, observing with interest the five enemy vessels flying before them.

Just before 1:00 p.m., the British fired their first salvoes at a range of more than eight nautical miles, 16,000 yards. These fell short, but in 15 minutes they began to straddle *Leipzig*, the rearmost ship in the German line. At this point, von Spee ordered his light cruisers to attempt escape. Sturdee had foreseen this manoeuver. Without further orders, his armoured and light cruisers scattered in pursuit of the smaller German ships. Von Spee led *Scharnhorst* and *Gneisenau* toward *Invincible* and *Inflexible*.

What followed was in essence a mirror of Coronel, with the weaker force attempting to close the range while the stronger and faster maintained its chosen distance. It was not easy because only a 3,000 yard range difference existed between Sturdee's 12-inch and von Spee's 8.2-inch guns. Hampered by clouds of smoke and vibration in the masthead directors, the British shooting was slow, ragged, and inaccurate. As the afternoon wore on Sturdee was forced to close the range and von Spee's already damaged vessels were able to open fire, straddling their targets with their third salvoes. The heavily armoured British ships were hit repeatedly, but their fighting value was not impaired.

In the midst of the action, a four-masted sailing ship appeared, with all sails set, and ran between the battle lines. According to a British officer: "A truly lovely sight she was, with every inch of canvas drawing as she ran free in the light breeze, for all the world like a herald of peace bidding the two lines of warships to cease the senseless destruction."

Sturdee's gunnery became more accurate and the German ships began to suffer severely. They went on firing with great accuracy, with their upper works in a shambles and raging fires visible through gaping holes in their sides. Von Spee's last signal to Maerker of *Gneisenau* was, "You were right after all," a reference to his advice not to approach the Falklands. At 4:17, *Scharnhorst* rolled onto its side and went down with all hands, propellers still rotating and flag still flying.

Gneisenau survived for another hour and a half. Untested at Coronel, Pochammer's damage control and firefighting parties were overwhelmed, as boilers and engines were wrecked and water poured through shell holes, trapping men in flooded and steam-filled compartments. Most of the gun crews were killed, but an occasional shot still rang out. At 5:40, with ammunition ex-

Invincible picking up survivors of Gneisenau.

hausted, Maerker ordered the ship scuttled. The survivors from the crew of 765 were ordered to abandon ship, and cheers rang out from *Invincible* until the captain ordered silence and brought his men to attention as *Gneisenau* disappeared. The British ships lowered their boats, but many men perished in the frigid waters before they could be picked up. In the end, 190 were saved. The admiral's sons were not among them. Out of respect for their stout resistance, Sturdee sent a congratulatory message to the senior survivor, Commander Pochammer.

Sturdee's cruisers overtook the fleeing *Leipzig* and *Nurnberg*, and sank them both. All but one of the colliers accompanying von Spee were captured. Thanks to turbine engines, *Dresden* escaped to lead a fugitive existence until 14 March 1915. Tracked down at Mas a Tierra by *Kent* and *Glasgow*, it was scuttled after a brief resistance. *Glasgow* was the only ship on either side to be involved from the beginning and to survive both battles.[4]

No Canadian ships were present at Coronel, but in *Canada's Navy, the First Century,* Marc Milner suggests that the battle may have been the most decisive in the history of the RCN. This hypothesis rests on the fact that it cost the navy four of the 20 members of its first officer entry, at least two of whom were marked out as having unusual potential. The idea gains additional credence when it is remembered that a classmate, William Maitland-Dougall, was also killed during the war. The composition of the RCN's senior leadership in World War II might well have been different had these five been among the small pool of officers who persevered through the interwar years. What that might have meant for the navy's achievements in the Battle of the Atlantic, and for its later development, is a fascinating subject for speculation, but in the nature of things, unknowable.

EPILOGUE

Painting in tribute to the lost midshipmen by Commander Frederick "Hamish" Berchem, Royal Canadian Navy, Retired.

The four midshipmen were memorialized in many ways, both public and private. Their families received posthumously awarded medals. The British government created a special memorial plaque, and the Canadian government established the Silver Cross, still awarded to mothers of sons and daughters lost in conflict.

Even before the war ended, the Fredericton chapter of the Imperial Order Daughters of the Empire (IODE) was named after Midshipman Hatheway. Cenotaphs in their home towns carry their names, recognizing them as the first of their service to die in World War I. The Maritime Command Museum in Halifax, the Yarmouth County

Museum and Archives and Fredericton's Historical Society Museum exhibit personal artefacts that belonged to the four midshipmen, which give glimpses into who they were as individuals. Their names are recorded in illuminated script in the first Book of Remembrance in the Memorial Chamber of the Peace Tower at Parliament Hill in Ottawa, and on the Commonwealth War Graves Sailor's Memorial in Halifax.

In 1953, a ship of the RCN marked the battle at its site, when HMCS *Ontario* paused for a brief service during a training cruise to South America.

On 1 November 1974, the anniversary of the battle which took their lives, the four were remembered when the new library at Royal Roads, the successor to the Royal Naval College of Canada, was named the Coronel Memorial Library. William Palmer's sister Gertrude, in her 80s, attended.

On 9 November 1915, a monument to Cradock was unveiled in York Minster in the admiral's home county of Yorkshire. The inscription concludes with a passage from the First Book of Maccabees:

> *God forbid that we should do this thing,*
> *To flee away from them.*
> *If our time be come, let us die manfully for our*
> *brethren*
> *And let us not stain our honour.*

Everything we know about Coronel and the Falklands testifies that this spirit inspired not only Cradock, but also the thousands on both sides who died there, including Midshipmen Malcolm Cann, John Hatheway, William Palmer and Arthur Silver.

ENDNOTES

CHAPTER 1: BEGINNINGS

1 *Niobe* was actually the largest ship the RCN ever possessed until the aircraft carrier *Magnificent* was transferred from the RN in 1948.

2 Forty years later military college cadets received the same 75 cents every week, still provided by their parents, but worth much less than the same sum in 1910.

3 THE RCN'S FIRST OFFICER TRAINEES
Cadets in CGS Canada, 1909-1910
J.W. Barron, A.T. Bate, C.T. Beard, V.G. Brodeur (Admiral WW II), P.B. German, P.W. Nelles (1st Chief of Naval Staff, WW II), W.R. Wright

First Entry, RNCC, 1911-1912 († : Lost in World War I)
R.I. Agnew, M.Cann†, H. Dand, L.J.M. Gauvreau, J.M.Grant, J.V. Hatheway†, H.J. Hibbard, G.C. Jones (2nd Chief of Naval Staff, WW II), D. Laurie, R.F. Lawson, W.M. Maitland Dougall†, D.B. Moffat, L.W. Murray (Commander, Canadian Atlantic Area, WW II), J.E. Oland, W.A. Palmer†, C.W. Reid, A.W. Silver†, H.R. Tingley, R.C. Watson, G.A. Worth, H.R. Yates

4 The widening of the Kiel Canal was scheduled to be completed in July 1914. Presciently, Admiral Fisher predicted that the event would signal that war was imminent.

5 Quoted in Hal Lawrence, *Tales of the North Atlantic*.

CHAPTER 2: THE UNCERTAIN TRUMPET

1 To stimulate national interest in its new navy, the German government named a large class of cruisers after inland towns where knowledge of maritime matters was minimal. Beginning in World War II, the RCN adopted the same practice for the same reasons.

2 Qingdao is now one of the Chinese navy's principal bases.

3 All personal anecdotes and direct quotations from Winston Churchill come from *The World Crisis*, his history of the First World War.

CHAPTER 3: A CUT FLOWER IN A VASE

1 William Palmer received the recall while boating on the North-west Arm with a young woman who later married his brother Frederick. He remarked to her "This means we are at war."

2 In *The Sea is at our Gates*, Cdr. Tony German indicates this discrepancy was due to a mistake by an admirality clerk.

3 It seems unlikely that after only two days on board his flagship, Admiral Cradock knew enough about the group to personally select two of them. However, he had always been interested in junior officer training and made a habit of associating with them on an informal basis. *Berwick*, with the Canadian mids, had been his flagship in Mexican waters in the autumn of 1913. Perhaps he had more direct knowledge of the young men than might have been expected.

4 At the outbreak of war, Cradock defaced the medal ribbon with blue ink, and thereafter referred to it as the Order of the Blue Ape.

5 At some unknown date *Karlsruhe* was destroyed by an internal explosion. In ignorance of this fact, significant British forces continued to search for some time, subtracting from the effort that might have been allocated to Cradock.

6 In marked contrast, the Germans apparently had little difficulty in making re-supply merchant vessels available at every anchorage at which von Spee's squadron stopped to coal.

7 In the early days of the war, off San Francisco, *Leipzig* very nearly encountered H.M.C.S. *Rainbow*, which had bravely sortied from Esquimalt. If the vessels had met there can be little doubt that it would have meant the end of the Canadian ship, such was the disparity in combat capability.

CHAPTER 4: AT THE GOING DOWN OF THE SUN

1 In an era of rapid change, later guns achieved greater ranges than their same calibre predecessors, and might even out-range earlier weapons of higher calibre. The range of the 8.2-inch main armament of *Scharnhorst* and *Gneisenau* exceeded that of *Good Hope's* 9.2-inch and *Canopus'* 12-inch by well over 1000 yards.

2 Anti-German feeling became so strong that the Royal family adopted the name "Windsor" instead of "Saxe-Coburg Gotha," and gave up all its German titles. The Battenbergs anglicized their name to Mountbatten. Prince Louis' youngest son, Lord Louis Mountbatten of Burma, held his father's old post of First Sea Lord from 1954 to 1959. His nephew, Prince Philip Duke of Edinburgh, is the Queen's consort.

3 A more modern and more powerful armoured cruiser than *Good Hope*, *Defence* had an experienced regular force crew and should have been a match for one of von Spee's large cruisers, leaving *Good Hope* and *Monmouth* to take on the other. Cradock believed that in such an encounter the odds would have been in his favour.

4 Providentially for Lieutenant Hirst, the rough seas made it impossible for him to transfer to *Good Hope*, thus saving his life.

5 Primitive as it was, the detection and jamming of enemy wireless communications in this encounter may be among the first recorded examples of what became known as electronic warfare, now a critical factor in all military operations.

6 *Glasgow* had been on the point of returning to England when war broke out. Among the South American souvenirs collected by the ship's company were 60 parrots. With the ship going into action it was decided to release the birds to fend for themselves. Stunned by the noise, they fluttered in the rigging and even perched on the hot barrels of the guns. Amazingly, 10 survived.

CHAPTER 5: FULL CIRCLE

1 The great encounter did not come until 31 May 1916, at Jutland, where the British suffered heavier losses than their opponents while failing to completely defeat them. But the severely damaged High Seas Fleet fled to port and never sailed to challenge the Grand Fleet again; instead, the Germans turned to unrestricted submarine warfare.

2 In the Cann letter, like the others, Hazen states that Malcolm Cann was specially chosen by Admiral Cradock, which is in conflict with the eyewitness account mentioned in Chapter 3 to the effect that only Silver and Palmer were selected by name, Cann and Hatheway by lot. If he knew this, Hazen nevertheless chose to tell all four families that their sons had been specially chosen, no doubt to soften the blow of their deaths.

3 Most analysts agree that this plan was the worst of the possible alternatives. Either the whole force should have been concentrated for a surprise attack at first light or only one light cruiser should have made the dawn reconnaissance, the remainder staying out of sight until the situation was clear.

4 One of *Dresden's* officers, Lieutenant Canaris, was responsible for the deception plans that allowed his ship to elude detection for so long. After the war he remained in the navy and became head of Hitler's intelligence service in World War II, while working secretly against the Nazis. He was executed after the failed attempt on Hitler's life in 1944.

PHOTO CREDITS

Maritime Command Museum: 7 (right), 7 (left and middle), 8, 11, 12, 15, 22, 23, 27, 33 (right), 41 (middle), 58; Maritime Command Museum, photo by Malcolm Cann: 14 (top, middle and bottom), 17, 18, 31; Author, courtesy Ila Vanrenen: 16 (right), 25 (middle) and 34 (right), 26, 28 (top and bottom), 29 (top and bottom), 34 (left), 41 (right), 42, and 55; National Archives: back cover (top) and 10 (bottom); Public Archives of Nova Scotia, Nottman Studio: 43; High resolution image provided from DND Navy Heritage Website www.navyheritage.forces.gc.ca): negative number DND Palmer- HS-6530, 9; DND - CN-6593, 19; HMSGood-Hope-03, 44; DNDSpee-1, 47; HMSGlasgow-03,49; HMSMonmouth-03,50; SMSScharnhorst-01,52; HMS-GoodHope-01,53; SMSDresden-03, 54; HMSGood-Hope-03, 60 (top); HMSMonmouth-03, 60 (bottom); SMSLeipzig-02, 65; SMSGneisenau-02, 67; SMSS-charnhorst-02,69; DND - Coronel-02, 70 SMSScharn-horst-03, 71; DND - Coronel-03, 76; DNDPalmer-8, 75 (right) and 78; DND: HS-6351A, 10 (top); N-22752, 13 (bottom); DND Navy Heritage website courtesy of Ila Vanrenen, nee Palmer, Australia: 16 (left and centre), front cover and 33 (left) DNDPalmer-4; Commander; Frederick Berchem, 88, The Speaker of the House of Commons, 75 (left).

ACKNOWLEDGEMENTS

This story could not have been told without the assistance of more people than I can properly acknowledge. Jamie Serran and Nadine Gates of the Yarmouth County Museum were most helpful in tracing records and mementoes of Malcolm Cann. In Fredericton, I am grateful to Ted Jones for essential guidance and interpretation, and to Ms. Connie Steeves of the IODE for much useful information on John Victor Hatheway. As always, the staff of Nova Scotia Archives and Records Management in Halifax were unfailingly co-operative and efficient.

Lt. Cdr. Graeme Arbuckle of the Directorate of History at NDHQ developed the Centennial Naval Heritage website, a comprehensive and user-friendly source of information, and was always "Ready, Aye, Ready" to help in other ways.

Over the years, Ms. Marilyn Gurney, Curator of the Maritime Command Museum, has compiled a written and photo record that was absolutely indispensable to my research, and she and her assistant Rick Sanderson went out of their way to make it available and help me interpret the information. They have my sincere gratitude.

Commodore (Ret'd) Mike Cooper, former chair of the N.S. branch of the Naval Officers Association of Canada, played a critical role in putting me in touch with Ms. Ila Vanrenen of Melbourne, Australia. A niece of mid William Palmer, she has preserved a treasure trove of letters and photographs that shed a very personalized light on the tragedy of Coronel, and I am deeply grateful for her generosity in making that unique resource available to me.

Finally, I owe a big debt to James Lorimer and the staff at Formac Publishing. Above all, Christen Thomas guided the sometimes frustrating production process with skill and good humour, and again earned my gratitude and admiration.

In thanking all those who contributed so much, I, of course, take full responsibility for any shortcomings in the final result.

BIBLIOGRAPHY

Bennett, Geoffrey. *The Pepper Trader* (Jakarta, Indonesia: Equinox Publishing, 2006).

Bennett, Geoffrey Martin. *Coronel and the Falklands*, (London: B.T. Batsford, 1962).
———. *Naval Battles of the First World War* (London, Penguin Books Ltd., 2001).

Boutilier, James A., Ed. *The RCN in Retrospect*, (Vancouver: UBC Press, 1982).

Churchill, Winston. *The World Crisis* (Toronto: The Macmillan Company of Canada Limited, 1923).

Corbett, Sir Julian. *Naval Operations* (London: Longmans Green and Co., 1920).

Cradock, Admiral Sir Christopher. *Whispers from the Fleet* (Portsmouth, Gieves: Masters and Seagrove Ltd., Second Edition, 1908).

German, Tony, Cdr. *The Sea is at Our Gates* (Toronto: McClelland and Stewart, 1990).

Gimblett, Richard, Marc Milner, Peter Haydon et al. *The Admirals* (Toronto: Dundurn Press, 2006).

Hickling, Vice-Admiral Harold. *Sailor at Sea* (London: William Kimber, 1965)

Hirst, Lloyd. *Coronel and After* (London: Peter Davies Limited, 1934).

Hough, Richard. *The Pursuit of Admiral von Spee* (New York: Harper & Row, 1969).
———. *The Great War at Sea, 1914-1918* (Oxford: Oxford University Press, 1983).

Howarth, David. *Famous Sea Battles*, (Toronto: Little Brown and Company, 1981).

Irving, John. *Coronel and the Falklands* (London: A.M. Philpot Ltd., no date).

Jane, Fred T., Ed. *Fighting Ships, Report of 1914* (New York: Arco Publishing Co. Inc, 1969).

Keegan, John. *Intelligence in War, Knowledge of the Enemy from Napoleon to Al Quaeda* (Toronto: Key Porter, 2003).

Lawrence, Hal. *Tales of the North Atlantic* (Toronto: McClelland and Stewart, 1985).

Massie, Robert K. *Castles of Steel* (New York: Random House, 2003).

Macintyre, Captain Donald. *The Thunder of the Guns* (London: Frederick Muller Limited,1959).

Manchester, William. *The Last Lion* (Boston and Toronto: Little Brown and Company, 1983).

Milner, Marc. *Canada's Navy, The First Century* (Toronto: University of Toronto Press Incorporated, 1999).

Pitt, Barrie. *Coronel and Falkland*, (London: Cassell,1960).
———. *Revenge at Sea* (New York, Stein and Day, 1960).

Pochhammer, Captain Hans. *Before Jutland*, Tr. H.J. Stenning (London: Jarrolds Limited, 1931).

Ruiz, Ramon Eduardo. *Triumphs and Tragedy, a History of the Mexican People* (New York: W.W. Norton & Company, 1992).

Spencer–Cooper, Cdr. H. *The Battle of the Falkland Islands* (London: Cassell and Company, 1919).

Thurston, Arthur. *Midshipman Malcolm Cann and his Three Midshipman Buddies.* (Yarmouth, Nova Scotia: Thurston Publications, 1989).

Tirpitz, Grand Admiral von. *My Memoirs* (New York: Dodd, Wood and Company, 1919).

Tucker. *The Naval Service of Canada, Volume I* (Ottawa: The King's Printer, 1952).

Walter, John. *The Kaiser's Pirates* (Annapolis: Naval Institute Press, 1994).

Warner, Oliver. *Great Sea Battles* (London: Hamlyn Publishing Group, 1968).

Winton, John. *An Illustrated History of the Royal Navy* (London: Salamander Books, 2000).

INDEX